MAKING WOOD DECOYS

MAKING WOOD DECOYS

Patrick Spielman

Sterling Publishing Co., Inc.   New York

Library of Congress Cataloging in Publication Data

Spielman, Patrick E.
  Making wood decoys.

  Includes index.
  1. Wood-carving—Technique.   2. Decoys (Hunting)
I. Title.
NK9704.S66 1982   745.593   82-50556
ISBN 0-8069-5476-0
ISBN 0-8069-5477-9 (lib. bdg.)
ISBN 0-8069-7660-8 (pbk.)

        13   15   17   19   ?0   18   16   14   12

Contents

Color pages A, B, C, D follow page 32.

Acknowledgments

I wish to express my sincerest gratitude to a distinguished group of decoy carvers from Door County, Wisconsin, who enthusiastically and generously afforded me their time, expertise, and assistance. Without their help, this book would not be a reality. With their kind permission, they graciously allowed me to photograph their excellent decoy sculptures, and in many cases also consented to my converting their works into plans, which are included in this book. I extend a very heartfelt thank you to this group of excellent decoy artists: Peter Bosman, Keith Bridenhagen, Bill Dehos, John Eriksson, Thomas Herlache, and Harold Schopf. Their combined efforts and beautiful decoys are certainly a distinct feature of this book.

A special note of credit and appreciation is extended to Keith Bridenhagen. He served not only as an advisor and consultant, but made many valuable contributions to this effort. I thank Keith for his thoughtful suggestions concerning content, his pen-and-ink drawings of various decoys, the decoy samples he designed and executed especially for this book, and his patience during our long photo sessions.

I am also appreciative of the following companies, which provided photo illustrations and technical information: Adjustable Clamp Co. (Illustrations 52, 53), Buck Bros., Inc. (Illustration 32), Dremel Div.–Emerson Electric Co. (Illustration 143), Ebac of America (Illustration 16), Foredom Electric Co. (Illustration 43), Great Northern Decoy Co. (Illustrations 3, 4), Leichtung, Inc.

(Illustrations 2, 22, 33, 34, 41, 144, 148), Lewis Tool and Supply Co. (Illustration 145), Panavise (Illustration 39), Parker Paint Co. (Illustration 164), and Sand-Rite Mfg. Co. (Illustration 46).

Thanks to the following individuals who in various ways also helped: Ronnie Hanson, Wayne Harmann, James Hicks, Jon Kordon, John Lewis, Les Meyer, Charles Nurnberg, Don Podraza, Ross Rehr, Martin Schamus, Brigitte Seagard, Orville Voeks. And, finally, thanks to my wife Patricia, for her supportive "tolerance," and thank you to my daughter and typist, Sherri Spielman.

Patrick Spielman

Illus. 1. This unusual log sculpture created by John Eriksson in wormy butternut exemplifies the unique art of the wood decoyist and the special properties of real wood.

Introduction

Real wood decoys have become so popular they are now objects of much commercialization. Most of the old, authentic, decoys have long been snatched up at flea markets, antique shows, and auctions. Today, decoy collectors actively buy and trade old wooden decoys and seek out new, freshly carved ones. (See illustration 1.) Interior decorators love them, for decoys add a special nostalgic touch and create that country look so popular in recent years. Mail-order gift catalogs, furniture stores, and gift shops now feature real wood decoys that have been factory produced on carving machines. And, for the less affluent buyer, "genuine wood-grained," cast-plastic decoys are now arriving on the scene.

The woodworker and sportsman-hobbyist can buy do-it-yourself decoy carving kits from a growing number of companies. These are great for beginners, for those with limited work space, and for those with few tools. Decoy kits come in a wide range of duck species and sizes and are available at various stages of completion. In some kits, the ducks are precarved, with

Illus. 2. This carving kit comes all pre-carved, requiring only minimal work before finishing or painting.

only sanding and finishing remaining to be done. (See illustration 2.) Others provide the roughed-out block; the buyer does all the carving and finishing or painting. (See illustrations 3 and 4.)

Real handmade wood decoys are much in demand because people appreciate the artistic work and skill conveyed by the decoy maker. Sportsmen enthusiastically discuss decoy qualities (or lack of them) relative to shape, style, and detail. Almost any block fashioned to somewhat resemble a duck seems to find a market. A handmade wood decoy has a special character, imparted not only by the talents or limitations of the artist, but also by the natural, unique qualities of the wood itself.

The state of the art today is almost unbelievable. There are professional and contest carvers whose works are exact reproductions. You are sure that their wood decoys can quack and fly away. (See illustration 5.) These realistic decoys are proportioned to every minute detail, and are painted precisely, feather by feather, to duplicate nature's own colors.

This advanced level of decoy work requires considerable patience and research, and it consumes a lot of time. There are very few carvers who can attain the elite status of decoy master. It involves intensive practice, effort, and an intimate association with the wild fowl they are creating in wood. Carvers of this fraternity also work from many wildlife references and are guided by the writings of experts such as Burk and LeMaster.

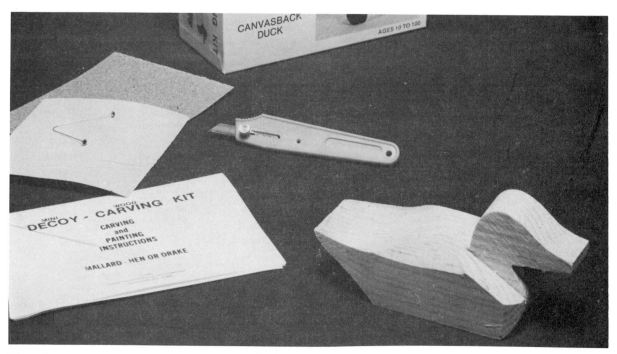

Illus. 3. These inexpensive miniature decoy kits provide a rough-sawn pine block, knife, sandpaper, glass eyes, and instructions.

Illus. 4. These completed kit-made mini-decoys are only 6″ (15.25 cm) long. Canvasback is shown above and mallard below.

Illus. 5. This preening hen teal decoy by Thomas Herlache is an excellent example of advanced realistic carving. Note how every intimate detail is recreated (yes, all in wood) to achieve this lifelike look.

This book is essentially for the beginner and the amateur woodworker. It is for those of us who admire and fondle every wood decoy within reach, while thinking, "I'd like to give this a try." *Making Wood Decoys* will guide you from the very beginning stages—from selecting wood and shaping it, right up to and including the basics of feather carving, finishing, and painting decoys. The majority of decoys featured are essentially simple decorative ones. Even with few details, they can be very beautiful when naturally finished. Also included are a number of plans and photos of decoy projects to challenge the experienced wood-carver. Very beautiful decoys can be made from low-cost, often readily available, woods with tools commonly owned by the average woodworker.

1

Woods for Decoys

One of the most serious concerns of the would-be decoy carver is: "Where do I get properly dried wood of suitable size?" (See illustration 6.) This chapter will deal with this fundamental problem, and offer some solutions and alternatives.

Almost any species of wood can be used to make a decoy. (See illustration 7.) Some are much easier to work and much better looking than others. There is a group of so-called "beautiful" furniture woods exhibiting that desirable appearance often referred to as figure (pretty-grain pattern).

Illus. 6. Solid wood body blocks. Left: sugar pine, right: Douglas fir. Note the fine, uniform grain of the sugar pine as compared to that of the fir block. Pine will carve much more easily, however, the Douglas fir can be used to make a primitive decoy as shown in illustration 7.

13

Illus. 7. This simple, primitive-looking decoy by the author was made from an inexpensive, knotty Douglas fir timber. It was contoured only enough to look like a duck, and is without detail. Texture was achieved after rough-carving by charring the surfaces with a propane torch. It was then worked with steel wool and rubbed clean with a terry cloth. This technique works well on fir, because of its very coarse grain. Otherwise, fir is a very poor choice for finely crafted decoys because it is hard to work.

These are good choices for decoys intended have a natural, transparent finish. The problem is buying the wood properly dried in the required thickness, or drying it yourself, if you can get your hands on it locally.

Wood is generally a small investment, regardless of price, compared to the labor that goes into it. The first-time carver may be putting himself through self-imposed torture if he selects poorly seasoned wood, or a hardwood which is difficult to control in carving. This is especially true if you have a minimum of power tools and intend to ''whack'' out a decoy with only a chisel and a knife. Don't laugh. It can be done with these basic tools, but tools and techniques will be covered later.

Additional considerations in the selection of a particular wood are, for the most part, determined by the desired end result. Will your decoy be painted, stained, or have natural transparent finish? Will it be a working decoy—that is, one you actually shoot over, or will it be a permanent ornament for your mantel or coffee table? Obviously, you would not select a beautiful, furniture-grade wood for a painted working decoy. Furthermore, wood for working decoys need not be as dry as wood to be used for an indoor display piece.

There are many species of wood to chose from. Check with woodworkers and carvers in your own locality to find out what they use, why they use it and where they obtain it. A brief discussion of some generally suitable woods follows:

REDWOOD is an ideal choice for easy carving. It is soft—maybe a little too soft—but it is easily cut with sharp tools. Redwood is available at most building-supply centers in 1- and 2-inch (2.5- and 5-cm) nominal thicknesses. Better grades are virtually perfectly uniform from piece to piece and free of knots and other defects. Some heavy timbers, such as 4 by 4's (10 × 10 cm) and larger sizes, may also be available, but timbers are more often of a construction grade, meaning that knots or an oblique grain may be present. Redwood is considered an expensive building material, but for the novice carver it may be a very good buy. The only disadvantage I can think of is its lack of character. Its grain pattern (figure) borders on monotony.

PINE (See illustration 6.) There are many different species within the pine family, but only two recommended for carving—sugar pine and white pine. Sugar pine is by far the better choice. Its uniform fibres cut easily and cleanly with or across the grain. It has subtle but pleasing figure that is easily enhanced with stains. Sugar pine allows the carver to achieve beauty along with fine detail. It seasons with minimal warpage or checking.

White pine is similar to sugar pine in appearance, uniform texture, straight grain, ease of use, and high stability once properly dried. Pines make beautiful decorative decoys when finished with transparent naturals, stains, or paint. Pine is available in 1- and 2-inch (2.5- and 5-cm) thicknesses at most building-supply sources. It is generally available kiln-dried in thicknesses up to 6 in. (15 cm). Some carvers' supply sources sell even thicker pine.

BASSWOOD is a very good carving wood, but it has virtually no figure. It is straight grained. Basswood shrinks substantially in width and thickness during drying, otherwise it holds its dimension well once dried. Basswood is a good choice for painted decorative decoys.

WHITE CEDAR was probably the number-one choice wood for working decoys in years past. It is very lightweight and durable, with good overall working qualities (See illustration 8.) In areas where white cedar grows, such as in northeastern Wisconsin, it remains a popular carving wood, but it is more and more difficult to obtain in other parts of the country. Like pine, white cedar is light in color and it has a subdued figure that comes alive when stained. White cedar is comparatively fast to air-dry, and it shrinks little in the process. White cedar is commonly marketed today as rustic fencing, poles, and posts because of its resistance to decay. Your local building-products supplier may have white cedar on hand in the form of wood fencing or posts. Either could be a very good purchase.

MAHOGANY is an imported wood with excellent carving qualities. Most mahoganies have uniform grain, freedom from defects, uniform texture, and dimensional stability. Mahogany is expensive and available in thicker sizes from hardwood specialty suppliers. I'm not thrilled with natural-finished mahogany decoys because of the "blah," monotonous figure of the wood, but it is great for carving.

WALNUT has all the desirable qualities, including appearance, workability, color, and figure. (See illustration 9.) Woodworkers love everything about it except the price—it's very expensive! It is also difficult to obtain dry in thick dimensions.

Illus. 8. Chunks of white cedar. Note the checks radiating toward the pith. As a general rule when using a block containing the pith center, remember that the wood will usually crack from the side which is closest to the pith as shown at the right.

Illus. 9. This is a PEG-treated walnut decoy, made by Ronnie Hanson. Holes were drilled into the body from the bottom to relieve stresses and increase the surface area for the PEG treatment. Note the unusual diagonal grain direction, which is only possible with a PEG-treated block.

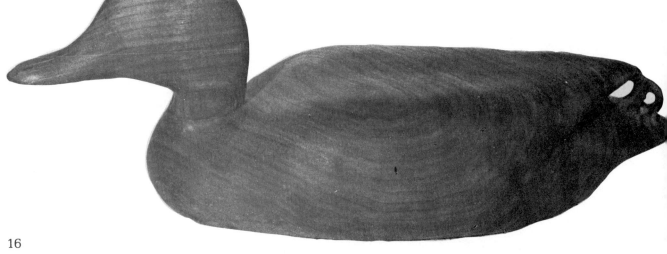

CHERRY, too, is a beautiful wood. It is harder than walnut and requires extreme care in drying to prevent cracking and distortion. As a rule, I don't recommend cherry or similar dense hardwoods such as plum, apple, pecan, and oak for solid, one-piece decoy bodies. However, these woods are used by experienced carvers and they would be satisfactory for decoys of hollow, and/or laminated construction.

BUTTERNUT is a hardwood with many admirable qualities. Most of the decoys illustrated in this book with natural transparent finishes are made of butternut. It's fairly fast and easy to dry. (See illustration 10.) Butternut has grain similar to walnut, but the color is more mellow, a brownish tone. It is softer and less dense than walnut and somewhat more difficult to carve. Tools must be extremely sharp to cleanly sever the fibres. It tends to fuzz in sanding, requiring more work in finishing, but when done properly the results are more than dramatic. In our area "wormy butternut" is very popular with carvers. (See illustrations 11, here, and 15, on page 22.) The wormy condition is caused by the larvae (worm stage) of the powder beetle. The worm channels actually reduce internal stresses, speed drying, and produce a special, rustic effect not otherwise possible.

Illus. 10. This completely solid, one-piece decoy of butternut made by Bill Dehos was very carefully dried to avoid cracking. Note the especially unusual figure pattern obtained with a block containing the pith center of the wood.

Illus. 11. This wormy butternut, almost to the point of "punky decay," would be discarded by most woodworkers. However, it can be worked into unusual decorative decoys.

SOFT MAPLE is used commercially by a number of machine carvers with excellent results. It is much easier to work than the other species of the hard maples which are very heavy, dense, and prone to checking and cracking while drying.

CHESTNUT is an extremely beautiful American decoy wood. It appears most frequently as "wormy chestnut." Like butternut, it has coarse texture, it is moderately light in weight, seasons well, and is easily worked with tools. Chestnut is a beautiful brown, highly figured wood. It may not be easy to obtain in many parts of the country since it is now almost extinct. It was attacked by a blight in the early 1900's. Today's supply comes mostly from dead, standing timbers that have endured over the years in the Appalachian Mountains, surviving because of great natural resistance to decay of its heartwood. It is sold in wood specialty supply houses.

TUPELO is sometimes referred to as black gum. A species marketed as water tupelo or swamp tupelo is the preferred wood of many professional and contest decoy carvers. The wood has fine, uniform texture, providing easy and predictable carving performance. This species grows principally in the Southeastern United States. It is now available, by mail order, especially for professional decoy carvers.

JELUTONG comes from Malaya. The wood is white or straw colored with no apparent difference between its heartwood and sapwood. Jelutong has a fine even texture with straight grain. It is very easy to season with minimal splitting or warping. Other positive qualities include ease of use and satisfactory gluing. However, it may be difficult to stain.

DRYING AND SEASONING YOUR OWN WOOD Serious wood-carvers eventually seek out their own sources for wood. Their major problem is drying it. Getting your hands on available "found" wood is fairly easy. With a little creative searching, wood-carvers can find good carving wood in firewood piles, in old posts (see illustration 8), branches of tree limbs from parks, construction sites, road and housing developments, and so on.

As a general rule, thicker wood must be dried more slowly than thinner pieces, and hardwoods dried more slowly than softwoods. As wood dries, moisture must move from its center to the surfaces. As water leaves the wood, shrinkage and internal stresses set up within the material.

Thick pieces of green wood should be air-dried very slowly over a very long period of time—maybe two to four years, depending upon the thickness and species. Fresh-cut wood should have its ends coated with paraffin to restrict the rapid escape of moisture out of the end grain. Large-diameter logs should be split lengthwise along the center pith of the log. Do not dry wood by putting it in direct sunlight. Keep it under a roof, but in a well ventilated area. One carver I know uses an old corn crib, which allows the air to circulate freely through his stacks of blocks.

The drying time will vary among species and thicknesses. Observation and experience are the keys. Some experienced carvers can tell when air drying is complete simply by observing the weight of the wood. Once the weight seems to be constant (after initial moisture loss), move it indoors but away from direct heat. It's probably best to place it in a basement for another 6 to 12 months. Before carving, move it to a warmer area, allowing it to reach the equilibrium with the moisture content of your surroundings.

Experienced carvers have numerous tricks and schemes for drying wood—far too many to all be discussed here. Some carve the wood green and then dry it slowly, storing the work in moist rags or in a plastic bag (with small slits in it) so the moisture does not escape too rapidly. Some take a green or partially dried chunk and boil it for several hours in water and then immediately work it. Another scheme I have heard of is to bake all the moisture out of the wood so it is bone dry. This method causes cracks, which the carver then fills in with carved wedges made to fit each crack. The theory is that the wood will again take on moisture from the air and swell up. The cracks will then reclose tightly against the wood filler wedges.

Obviously, every system has some questionable aspects to it. The objective is to get the moisture content of the wood in equilibrium with the surrounding air. That is the point at which the wood will neither gain nor lose moisture. In most parts of the United States the moisture content of wood for indoor use should be six to eight percent to be in equilibrium with the surrounding air.

SOME THOUGHTS ABOUT CRACKS AND OTHER DEFECTS Most people do not want to purchase a decoy if it is cracked or has other separations in the wood. However, checking and cracking are as natural to wood as are worm holes, knots, swirly grain, and color variation. I really don't think small cracks or slight checks seriously detract from naturally finished decoys. Large ones—yes. Once the decoy has been through a year of changes from dry indoor winters to humid summers it is unlikely any further cracking will develop. Knots and other defects should not be located in areas such as the eye or bill, where they would interfere with delicate carving jobs.

CHECKING THE MOISTURE CONTENT OF WOOD This is most easily and accurately determined with an instrument made especially for this purpose. (See illustration 12.) Lumber dealers, furniture and cabinet shops may have

Illus. 12. Test a piece of 3-inch (7.6-cm) sugar pine for moisture content with a moisture meter.

one they will loan you. There are several small, inexpensive, battery powered, moisture meters available. They start in price at around $100. Most measure the moisture down to six percent with remarkable simplicity and accuracy. They are calibrated so the moisture content of the wood being tested is read directly on the dial. These meters function by showing the relationship between the moisture and the electrical resistance in the wood. The dial or scale is activated when the two prongs are driven into the wood and a current flows between them. To make a good test, several readings should be taken at various locations in the chunk of wood. Always insert the contact pins so the current flows from one pin to the other in a direction that is parallel with the grain.

LAMINATED DECOYS The lamination technique involves gluing pieces of thinner materials to make one larger item. (See illustrations 13 and 14.) This method should be explored, especially for painted decoys. Since it's easy to purchase dry boards in 1″ and 2″ (2.5 and 5 cm) thicknesses or to dry these thicknesses, much time and worry about cracking is eliminated. Furthermore, blocks of any size can be made. Lamination is also worth considering for other unpainted decorative decoys. I personally feel that glue lines detract from the appearance of such decoys, but if you have no other immediate choice, why not? If you can obtain good, thicker dry boards, such as 2″-thick (5-cm) ones, there will obviously be fewer glue lines. On the other hand, decoys that are to be painted can be built up of many layers of wood in any available sizes and the glue lines can run either horizontally or vertically. (See illustrations 13 and 14.)

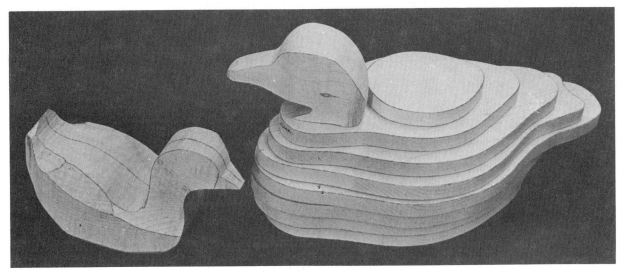

Illus. 13. Rough-sawn blocks. A solid, one-piece decoy is on the left, and horizontally laminated ½-inch (1.3-cm) boards on the right. (See page 48 for plans and details for hollow-laminated construction.)

Illus. 14. A vertically laminated goose decoy. This work-in-progress by Keith Bridenhagen will be painted so various colors and wood-filled defects will be completely hidden in the finished product.

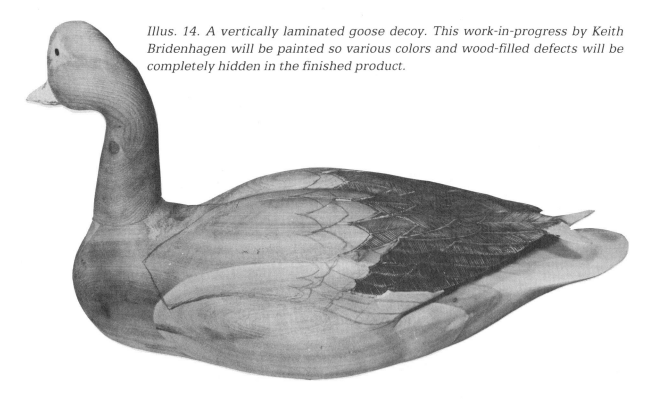

Illus. 15. Hollowing out the bottom reduces overall thickness, advances final drying, and relieves internal stresses.

HOLLOW CONSTRUCTION This technique involves ''digging'' out the inside of the decoy body so that at any point in the body the wood does not exceed 1 to 1½" (2.5 to 3.8 cm) of stock thickness. (See illustration 15.) The hollowing technique can also be employed with the laminating method. Refer to illustrations 54 and 55 on page 47, and illustrations 72 and 73 on page 58.

SOLID CONSTRUCTION In my opinion, the solid, one-piece body for the unpainted, decorative decoy is still the most beautiful. PEG (*polyethylene glycol*) treatment and dehumidification are two fairly new wood seasoning processes which may be of interest to serious wood-carvers.

PEG TREATMENT PEG refers to a chemical seasoning process in which freshly cut green wood can be utilized. (See illustration 9.) In this system the wood is worked to a rough size and shape while it is still in its green state. It is then immersed in a solution of PEG and water for a specified time which is determined by thickness and species. Then it is air-dried or force-dried in a conventional oven only to the point where the outer surfaces are dry. The PEG locks the moisture inside. PEG-treated wood is somewhat more difficult to finish than conventionally dried wood. However, PEG provides the opportunity for much faster use of green wood than conventional wood-drying methods allow. Refer to my book, *Working Green Wood with PEG* (Sterling Publishing Co., Inc.), for complete information and instructions about using PEG for green-wood carving.

Illus. 16. The Ebac dehumidifier measures 12½ inches (31.75 cm) wide, 15⅜ inches (39 cm) deep, and 20½ inches (52 cm) high. The power requirement is 120 volts, and it can extract up to 3 gallons (11 litres) over a 24-hour period.

DEHUMIDIFICATION This is a new system recently introduced in this country to dry wood. Only very recently has this type of equipment become available for the home craftsman and small-quantity wood users. (See illustration 16.) Briefly, the dehumidification system lowers the vapor pressure of the surrounding air, and thus encourages evaporation by removing moisture from the air surrounding the wood. The system requires the construction of a simple, inexpensive, enclosed chamber to contain the lumber and equipment. According to the manufacturer, a home craftsman can dry his own hardwood timbers, in the 3"- to 5"-thickness range, (7.6- to 12.7-cm) at a rate of about ¼ percent moisture content per 24 hours. Poplar or basswood that is 4" thick (10 cm), for example, can be dried from 28 percent to 8 percent in about 80 days. This is accomplished at a current electrical-rate cost of less than 3 cents per board foot. For more information, contact Ebac of America, 1715 North Sherman Drive, Indianapolis, Indiana 46218.

Illus. 17. A stylized pintail in natural-finished butternut by Bill Dehos.

Illus. 18. A mallard drake by John Eriksson. Here a little basic feathering is included along with some stain to indicate the bird's prominent coloring. The stained areas were achieved by mixing regular food coloring with clear finish and applying it directly to the raw wood.

2

Design, Copying, and Stylizing

Before undertaking any woodworking project, the craftsman should give some conscious thought and effort to developing the overall design or plan. At the same time, he must consider his skill or previous experience, along with the materials and tools available to handle the job. Often beginners take on advanced, complex projects, become discouraged, and fall short of their expectations. In decoy making, as with all woodcrafts, there is a broad range of challenges from simple to complex.

In general, handmade wood decoys fall into these basic groups:

1. Working decoys: Used for hunting, these are crudely painted and purely functional.

2. Simple decorative decoys: These have minimal detail work and a natural or painted finish. (See illustration 17.)

3. Detailed decorative decoys: These decoys have additional feathers and may also be naturally finished or painted. (See illustration 18.)

4. Realistic decoys: These creations reproduce live ducks in every exacting detail, and involve extremely precise paint jobs. (See illustration 19.)

Most decoy carvers are copiers; they must be in some degree to end up with something recognizable as a duck. Some decoy carvers pride themselves on their ability to copy precisely a specific decoy of historical or other significance. They proudly call themselves counterfeiters. The purist makes the realistic decoy, attempting to copy in wood Nature's features in intimate detail. Unquestionably, this is the work of the most skillful and experienced carver.

Some decoy makers believe that if it's not an exact duplication of a famous existing decoy, or not an exact copy of a live duck, it's not good. If you allow yourself to be so intimidated, you will soon be discouraged. In reality, your first decoy will be less than perfect when viewed by such carvers. Remem-

Illus. 19. This hooded merganser drake by Harold Schopf has every detail of an actual duck precisely represented.

ber, carvers in this realm are not only wildlife experts, but they do exhaustive research and possess a mastery of technique. They consistently study wildlife photos, books, and even have birds frozen, preserved, or stuffed for on-hand models.

That's great for those so inclined and dedicated to perfection. Someday you may become so involved in making realistic decoys that you will establish similar standards and self-expectations. However, right now you can make beautiful decoys of simple designs without being a wildlife expert. If you don't attempt more than you can handle, your first decoy will turn out just fine, I assure you. The second will be even better, and so on.

The real beauty of making wood decoys is that if the head should turn out a little smaller than intended or one side a little fatter than the other, it is not necessary to fret or become discouraged. Simply take a quick look at other living creatures—including the human species. Some are short and fat and others tall and thin. There are all sorts of configurations among living things.

The hunters of days past carved their own working decoys without worrying about pretty looks. Their essential purpose was to make decoys that lured ducks within gun range. Exact shape, detail, and precise duplication of nature were not practical or necessary. Ducks in flight first saw the decoys at a distance. Once they were close enough to know they were deceived, it was too late. The decoy already had served its purpose.

Today the majority of decoys made are for decorative and ornamental purposes, rather than actual decoying. Yours need not be an exact duplica-

Illus. 20. The author's "unfinished" decoy. Liking the rustic look of carved texture, the work was stopped at this stage. Only a light sanding with very fine abrasive to highlight the knife marks was done.

tion of a duck. Obviously it should be a block worked to a somewhat recognizable shape. (See illustration 20.) Your decoy will be whatever you plan it to be and say it is. It is your interpretation and your expression—a three-dimensional statement all your own.

To help you get started you may want to copy or use as guidelines some of the plans and photos included in this book. You can attempt to copy them closely or design them otherwise. Departure is encouraged—be it by plan or by accident! However, if you are just a first-timer you may like a little guidance—a push so to speak. Consequently, if you are accustomed to the step-by-step approach, the following paragraphs and the remaining chapters will be of help to you. Your own style, technique, and skills will evolve naturally.

Begin by enlarging the selected drawing using the graph-square (or grid) system to make your full-size patterns. (See illustration 21.) Patterns can be enlarged or reduced simply by using squares of the appropriate size. Draw the same number of squares as are given on the original. Make the pattern by reproducing the lines and drawing in each corresponding square, one at a time, until the pattern is reproduced to the desired size. Other techniques and devices can be used to simplify pattern work, such as the inexpensive pantograph shown in illustration 22.

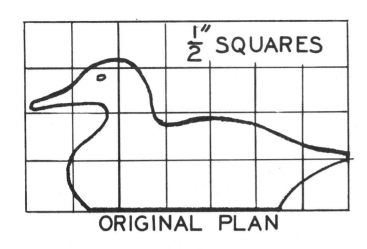

$\frac{1}{2}''$ SQUARES

ORIGINAL PLAN

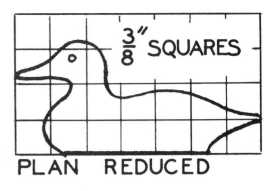

$\frac{3}{8}''$ SQUARES

PLAN REDUCED

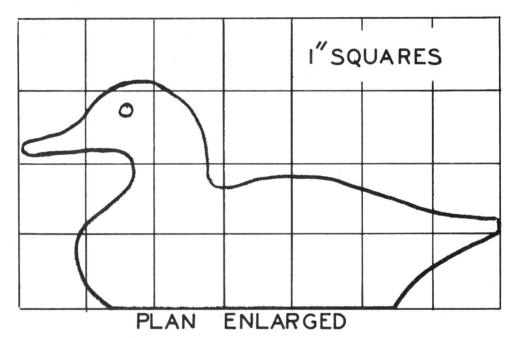

1" SQUARES

PLAN ENLARGED

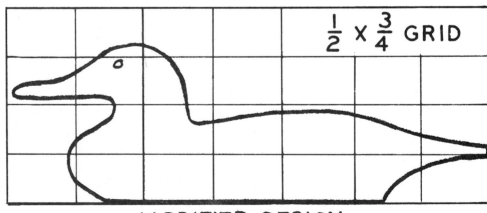

$\frac{1}{2} \times \frac{3}{4}$ GRID

MODIFIED DESIGN

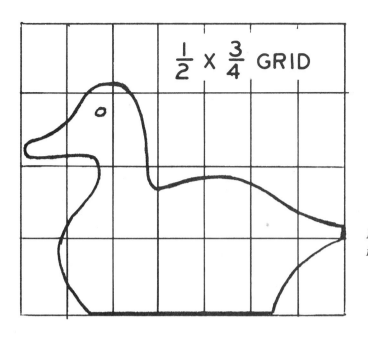

MODIFIED DESIGN

Illus. 21. Enlarging, reducing, and stylizing with the grid system.

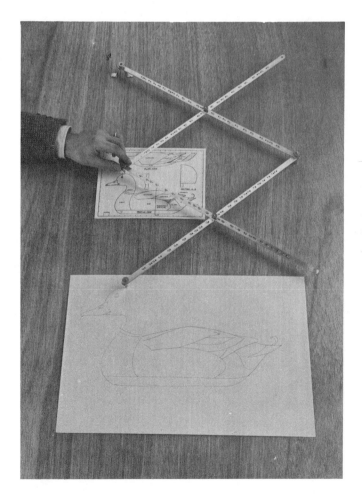

Illus. 22. A pantograph will enlarge and reduce patterns. To use, simply set the ratio and trace the original plan. A lead pointer makes the new-sized plan.

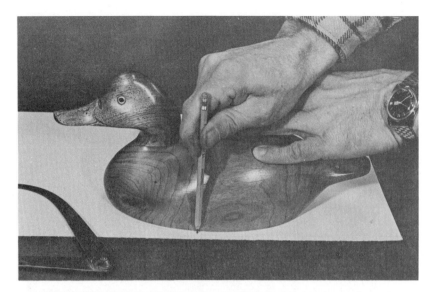

Illus. 23. Tracing the top view of the body.

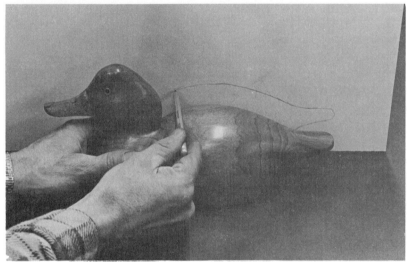

Illus. 24. Tracing the profile view of the body.

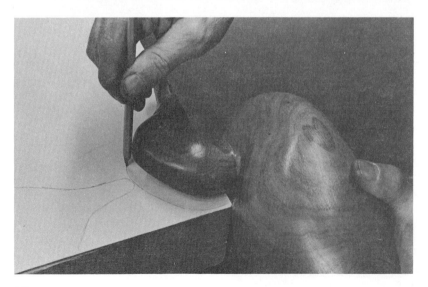

Illus. 25. Copying the head profile.

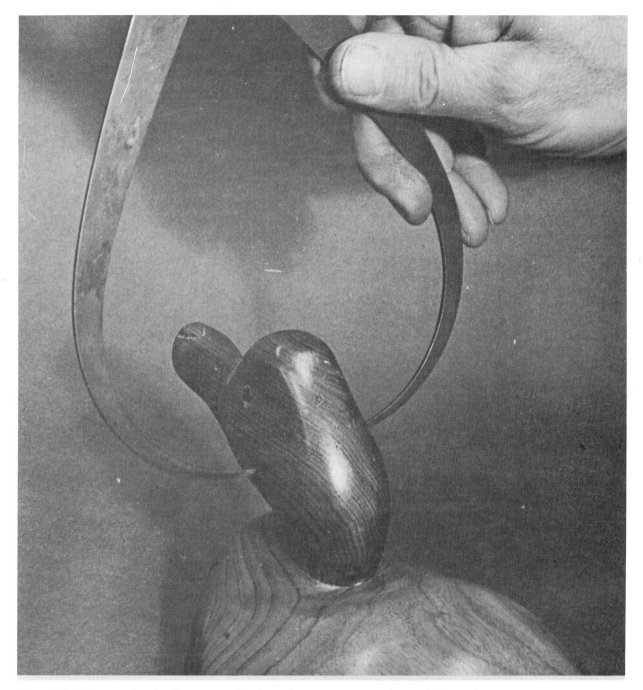

Illus. 26. Use a pair of calipers to check various representative points against your tracing. Modify your drawing accordingly.

COPYING A READY CARVED DECOY You may one day want to copy someone else's decoy as closely as you can. Illustrations 23, 24, and 25 show a crude but fairly effective method for developing the patterns. Use a pair of calipers to check sizes at various representative points. (See illustration 26.)

Illus. 27. Templates are used to check shapes and contours.

If you trace on paper or cardboard you can scissor-cut the patterns and hold them against the original in template fashion. (See illustration 27.) By trial and error you will come very close to the decoy you are copying.

MODIFYING AND STYLIZING PATTERNS It's often fun to intentionally change the profile shape of a plan slightly or, perhaps, even dramatically, but still maintain some semblance of representative style and proportion. This can be done in the planning stages. Use a rectangular grid similar to the one shown at the bottom of illustration 21, rather than using a conventional square grid. By drawing everything all out first you will be able to preview the style change. If you like it, you have a ready pattern. If you don't, you can depart from it freehand. It is always a good idea to plan out your design on paper before going to wood.

A Gallery of Natural and Painted Decoys

Two-piece hollow-bodied bluebill in oil-finished butternut by Patrick Spielman

Blue wing teal drake by Keith Bridenhagen

Calling loon in butternut by Harold Schopf

One-piece pintail in natural-finished butternut by Bill Dehos

Canvasback drake by Keith Bridenhagen

A

Pair of wood ducks in natural-
finished butternut
by John Eriksson

Mallard drake in stained and natural-finished
butternut by John Eriksson

Preening hen teal by Thomas Herlache

Preening Canadian goose by Harold Schopf

Ruddy duck drake by Thomas Herlache

B

Canvasback in stained pine by John Eriksson

Hooded merganser in butternut by Keith Bridenhagen

Old squaw drake in butternut by Keith Bridenhagen

Black duck drake by Keith Bridenhagen

Pair of canvasbacks in
butternut by Keith Bridenhagen

Mallard in stained white pine by Peter Bosman

Bluebill by Keith Bridenhagen

Curlew in butternut by Harold Schopf

One-piece cinnamon teal of a butternut burl by Bill Dehos

Solid-bodied bufflehead in cherry by Keith Bridenhagen

3

Basic Tools and Equipment

In decoy work, as in most other crafts, you can indulge yourself with all the mechanical tools you could ever want. The important questions are: What can you afford? Just how sophisticated do you want to be? The neat thing about decoy carving is that you can equip yourself with the essentials for about $15 or less at the local hardware store. For speed, convenience, and efficiency you can invest a great deal of money. But having expensive, luxury tools does not necessarily ensure better quality decoys.

Before buying any special, expensive tools, talk to as many other carvers as you can. Find out what the advantages and limitations are of the tools they use. Most woodworkers generally share their opinions and techniques. This chapter will illustrate and briefly discuss a general selection of tools that can be used to make decoys. Included are some of the more essential items, along with a number of tools and machines that are nice to have. Instructions with regard to safety, general procedures for use, sharpening tools, and other maintenance are not included here. Most woodworking books cover this information in considerable depth. Space does not allow it to be covered again here, so check at your local library if you need this kind of information.

KNIVES A good, sharp knife is an obvious necessity. One similar to the knife shown in illustration 28 is a good choice. It has a blade similar to a pocketknife, which, in fact, would work equally as well should you have one. Whatever knife or other edge tools you intend to use, sharpness is of ultimate importance. Sharp tools save time, energy, and contribute immensely to the joy and personal satisfaction of carving—more than anything else.

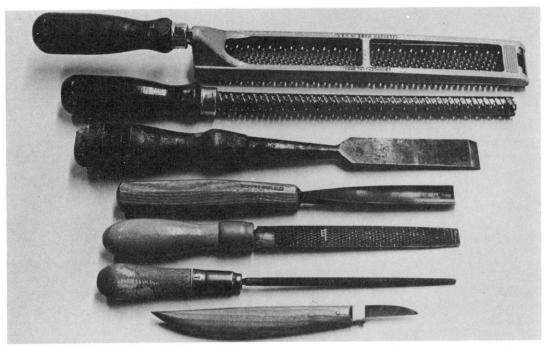

Illus. 28. A selection of basic carving tools includes Surform tools (at top), 1-inch (2.5-cm) chisel, medium gouge, one-half-round and small round rasp, and a carving knife.

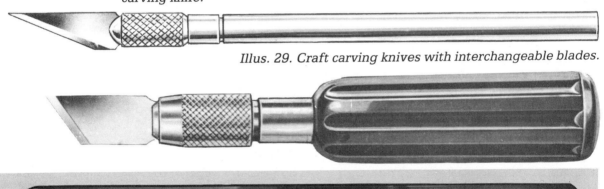

Illus. 29. Craft carving knives with interchangeable blades.

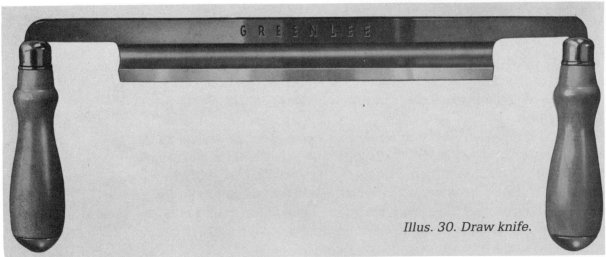

Illus. 30. Draw knife.

Replaceable-blade or craft knives are good for lots of jobs. (See illustration 29.) Smaller, pointed blades are more suitable for small, intricate detail work. The draw knife (illustration 30) is used by many decoy carvers for roughing out body shapes. I have one, but I don't use it at all for decoy carving.

CHISELS AND GOUGES A good chisel (illustrations 28 and 31) can be used for roughing out body blocks. If keenly sharpened, it can be used to slice thin shavings from convex surfaces. With a little practice, it can also be used, bevel down, to cut gradual inside curves. Carving gouges are used for forming concave surfaces. They may be purchased individually or in sets. (See illustration 32.) If buying only one, get one with a smaller to medium sweep (curved cutting edge), rather than a large one. A small-sweep gouge is more useful because it can be used to make cuts of a larger radius with multiple passes. A large gouge can only be used to make cuts of its own path size or larger.

RASPS AND FORMING TOOLS These are immensely useful for decoy work. Basically, all you need is a small half-round and a small round rasp. (See illustration 28.) The Stanley Surform tools (illustration 28) are very fast-cutting and are useful for removing a lot of material quickly. The new

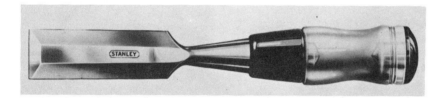

Illus. 31. A carpenter's butt chisel.

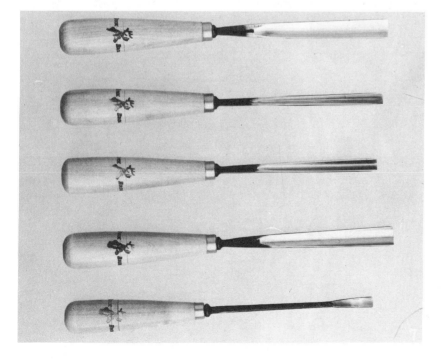

Illus. 32. Set of carving tools.

35

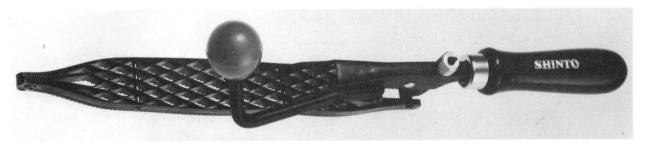

Illus. 33. The new Japanese saw rasp consists of ten two-sided hack blades. It cuts very fast and smooths surfaces as well.

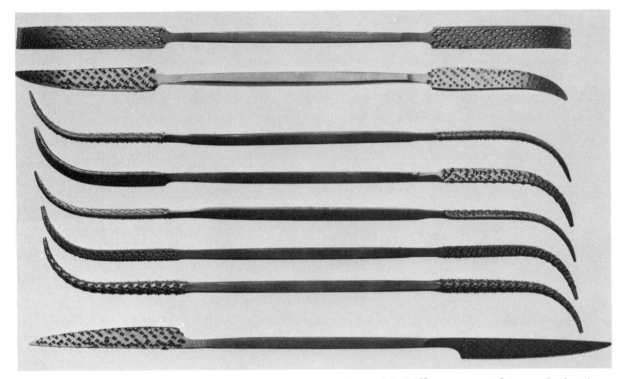

Illus. 34. Riffler rasp set for rough shaping.

Illus. 35. Coping saw.

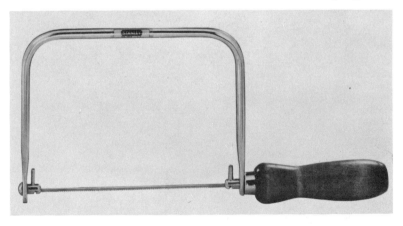

Japanese saw rasp (illustration 33) has similar advantages. Although rather expensive, a set of riffler rasps (illustration 34) does allow you to work in difficult-to-reach places. Riffler files are similar to riffler rasps but do not cut as fast. They are intended more for smoothing than stock-removal shaping jobs.

SAWS Decoy work often involves the need to cut irregular curves in thick wood. A coping saw (illustration 35) serves many uses in decoy work, but making cuts in thick wood with one is a tough task. The coping saw is almost a necessity, however; it is very useful for cutting off corners and making cuts underneath the wings.

A bandsaw (illustration 36) is obviously a very expensive item, but one the serious decoy artist can hardly get along without. If you don't have one, it is by far cheaper to pay another woodworker to use his, or to hire someone else to rough out your decoy bodies for you. If you intend to purchase a bandsaw one important consideration for decoy work is the stock thickness cutting capacity. One manufacturer makes a 14″ (35.6-cm) bandsaw with an optional extra-height cutting attachment. This accessory increases the thickness cutting capacity from 6¼″ (16 cm) to 12¼″ (31 cm).

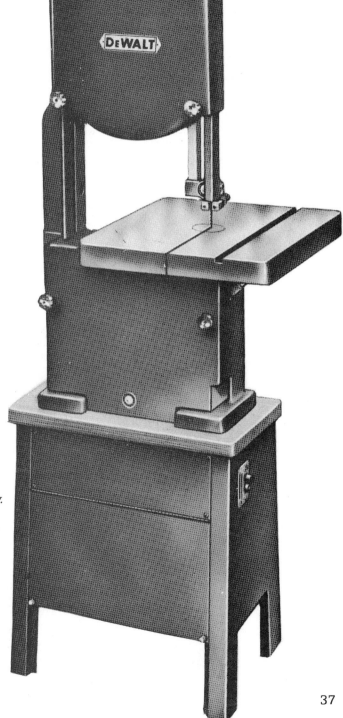

Illus. 36. Bandsaw.

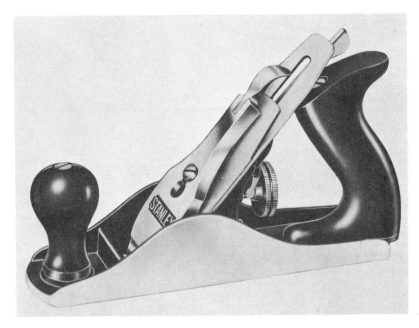

Illus. 37. (Left) Smooth plane.

Illus. 38. (Below) A jointer is useful for truing flat surfaces and for squaring.

Illus. 39. The base of a multiposition carvers' vise. When used with a work-holding fixturing head it will allow work to be swiveled or tilted to any convenient position.

Illus. 40. Two views of a fixturing head. The decoy is screwed to the head and then secured by the vise, which will hold the decoy in any position desired.

PLANING TOOLS You may need to smooth and flatten rough surfaces of boards to prepare them for gluing. A small, well-sharpened hand plane (illustration 37) can be used for this class of work. A jointer (illustration 38) is most helpful, doing the same job easier and faster.

VISES AND CLAMPS These tools hold the wood secure while you work it. Keith Bridenhagen, whose techniques are illustrated in Chapter 5, hardly ever clamps his work. He claims that too much time is lost in repositioning the work for each series of cuts or operations. Most of his carving and shaping is done while hand held. (Refer to pages 63–88.) However, I'm sure a vise would be very helpful to many people—especially to hold the work when both hands are needed.

A multiposition vise is considered by many carvers a basic necessity. Several ball-and-swivel-type vises are available to hold the duck in virtually any position. (See illustration 39.) With vises of this type, a fixturing head (illustration 40) must be screwed to the bottom of the block.

39

Illus. 41. Rotary rasp bits can be driven directly from power drills or through a flexible shaft as shown here.

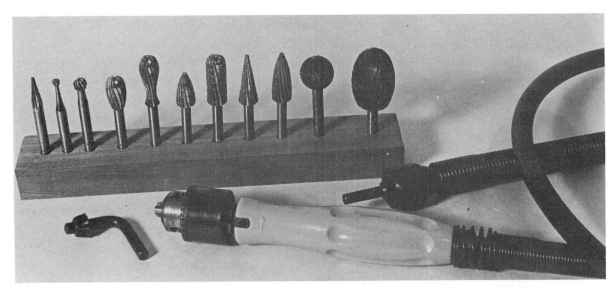

Illus. 42. Rotary burrs (files) with a flexible shaft and key-chuck hand piece.

ROTARY-POWERED CUTTING TOOLS These not only speed up the work but also take a lot of the sweat out of decoy making. The cutting is done with rotary rasps (illustration 41) or rotary filelike cutters sometimes called "burrs." (See illustration 42.) With these rotary tools proper grain direction becomes much less important than it does in carving with knife-edged tools. The bits or cutters may be driven directly from electric hand-drills or by flexible shafts coupled to a chuck-attached handpiece. Power sources can be portable drills, drill presses, or any suitable electric motor. Driving the cutters through flexible shafts allows for convenient one-handed control, which is not possible if the bits or cutters are chucked directly in a portable electric drill.

LIGHTWEIGHT POWER-CARVING TOOLS These are very popular with serious decoy carvers. (See illustrations 43 and 44.) Power tools such as these have collet-type chucks and can carry a wide variety of different miniature cutters, drills, wire brushes, sanders, saws, grinders, router bits, and so on. Small rotary tools can reach speeds as high as 35,000 RPM. Some types have the convenience of flexible shafts as standard equipment, and others can be coupled to a flexible shaft as an optional accessory. Both types can be operated with one hand, but usually two hands are used for optimum control in very delicate carving. The minipower bits have shank diameters of ⅛" (3.17 mm) or ³⁄₃₂" (2.38 mm), and the standard high-speed cutters are fairly inexpensive. Probably one of the best recent advances is the introduction of carbide cutters. These far outlast the high-speed steel ones.

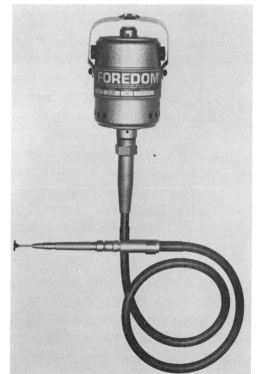

Illus. 43. The Foredom miniature power tool, Model R-7.

Illus. 44. The Dremel Moto-Tool kit.

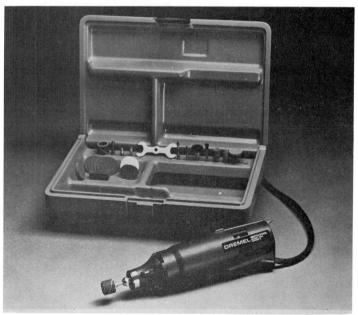

Illus. 45. A drum sander can be powered by an electric hand drill, a drill press, or it can be mounted to the shaft of an electric motor.

Illus. 46. Pneumatic drum sanding machine.

Illus. 47. Flap wheel sanders are available in various diameters, different widths, and with coarse-to-fine-grit abrasive.

SANDERS There are dozens and dozens of different devices and attachments available for power sanding. Large sanding machines such as vertical belt sanders and disc sanders found in many home shops can be used to remove corners from presawn rough body and head blocks. They can immensely speed up the job of getting the body close to the final contoured shape. With coarse abrasives, they remove wood quickly. However, they do not have much value for the final smoothing or finish-sanding. Likewise, drum sanders (illustration 45) with coarse abrasive will remove stock quickly to bring the inside contours close to the final shape. Drum-sanding attachments can be powered by a hand-held electric drill or drill press, or can be mounted directly to the shaft of an electric motor. Drum sanders are available in various diameters to grind away or form any concave contour. Very small, minidrum sanders are also available for use in flexible shaft and miniature power tools.

Professional carvers and sculptors use special flexible air-filled cylindrical sanders called pneumatic drum sanders. (See illustration 46.) This type of sander can be used for both stock removal and final smoothing, depending upon the grit of the abrasive sleeve. In use, air is pumped into the bladder of the drum so it will conform to the shape of the object being sanded. The air-filled drum gives with pressure, cushioning the work, allowing the abrasive to form to the contour of the work surface.

Flap wheel sanders (illustration 47) speed up final forming and reduce the amount of hand sanding required. These are fairly inexpensive and fairly efficient accessories. They perform essentially the same jobs as the flexible, air-filled (pneumatic) drum sanders. Flap wheels are available in various sizes, grits, and abrasive materials. They may be ordered to fit directly on a motor shaft or with a mandrel accessory for chucking in a handheld power drill or drill press. Cutting speed is controlled by the abrasive size as well as the amount of pressure exerted against the work.

MISCELLANEOUS TOOLS AND SUPPLIES These include the occasional use of drills (illustration 48), scissors, sanding-blocks, pencils, tape, paintbrushes, and so on. Most of these are fairly common household items. Very specialized tools (such as feather burners) used by experienced carvers and professionals will be discussed in Chapter 7.

Illus. 48. A hand drill with accessories is useful for many tasks in decoy making.

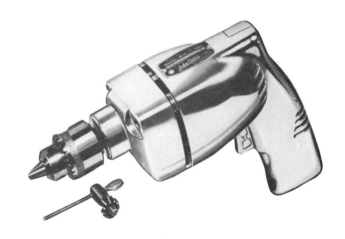

4

Making the Rough Blocks

Making the rough block involves all the preliminary work necessary to get the decoy ready for shaping to the final intended form. Careful preparation is essential to your overall success. Important matters pertaining to gluing and layout, and some tips on cutting and preliminary shaping are presented here. Most decoy makers prepare two blocks of wood; one for the body and another for the head. Some skilled carvers make the entire decoy—head and body—from one solid block. (See illustration 10, page 17, and illustration 17, page 24.) However, this method is not the common practice.

Since the body usually requires thick wood, it can be made of glued-up layers of thinner pieces or of one solid piece. Hollow construction techniques are often employed by contest decoy carvers to obtain a certain buoyancy in water. The same hollow-body method is used to make good working decoys, providing the additional advantage of reduced hauling weight. Particular decorative-decoy artists will also utilize the hollow-body method to reduce the mass of the wood, to reduce internal stresses in the wood which may cause cracks in further drying.

The following pages will illustrate and discuss techniques of preparing blocks for decoys of laminated solid bodies, laminated hollow bodies, and solid one-piece-body decoys. Any of these can be worked to rough shape by using ordinary hand tools or power tools.

CONSIDERATIONS FOR GLUING When building up body blocks consider the following:

1. Moisture content. All pieces within a glued-up block should be of uniform moisture content. Dry pieces mixed with wet ones will eventually equalize, causing shrinkage to the wet layers and expansion to the dry ones, resulting in a visible definition of each layer. (See illustration 49.)

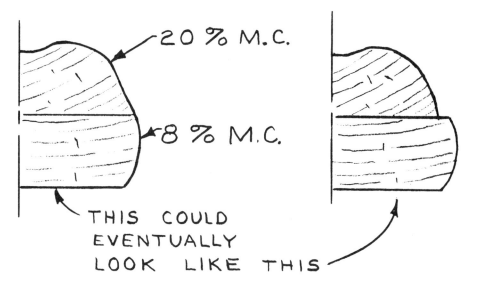

Illus. 49. Gluing together pieces of different moisture content eventually creates irregularities in the contoured surfaces.

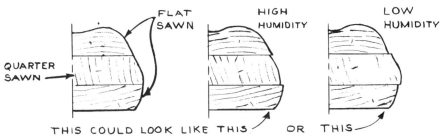

Illus. 50. Gluing together pieces of different grain can also cause surface irregularities with changes in atmospheric relative humidity.

2. Uniformity of grain. If possible, avoid gluing together quarter-sawn boards and flat-sawn boards. Flat-sawn pieces will expand and shrink in width more than quarter-sawn wood whenever changes in relative humidity occur. (See illustration 50.)

3. Plan the glue lines. That is, plan it so they end up in the least obvious part of the finished decoy. (See illustration 51.) This consideration is only important when the decoy is to have a transparent finish over natural or stained wood. Often, the contoured surface of the body runs gradually through or nearly parallel to the glue line, exposing a

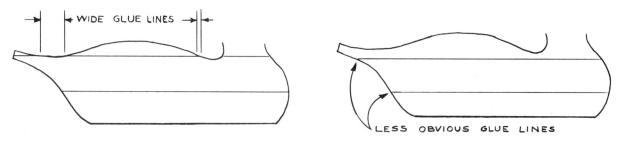

Illus. 51. When given a choice, plan your glue-up so the joints will be in the less evident areas of the finished decoy.

wide glue area. Glue resists taking stains and finishes. A poor finish is the result. This is a most important consideration which may necessitate changing the thickness and/or arrangement of the individual pieces before gluing them together.

4. Aligned grain direction.   Try to arrange pieces so that they all have their grain running in one direction to facilitate easier carving. Often, carving difficulties can be eliminated simply by checking the grain direction of each adjoining piece during glue-up.

5. Use of the correct glue.   Almost any type of woodworking glue can be used for decoys that will always be indoors. Working decoys should be assembled with waterproof glues such as marine-grade resin, resorcinol, or epoxy.

CLAMPING pressure can be applied with any suitable clamps available. (See illustrations 52 and 53.) If the individual pieces are cut flat and smooth, adequate clamping pressure can be obtained with weights such as concrete blocks or bricks set on top of the glued assembly.

*STACKED AND LAMINATED BOARD DECOY** Illustrations 54 and 55 show a rough-shaped, hollow-body decoy achieved by gluing up layers of

Photos and drawing based on a plan from September-October, 1944, issue of The Deltagram.

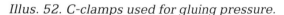

Illus. 52. C-clamps used for gluing pressure.

Illus. 53. Hand screw clamps.

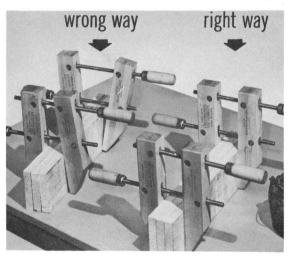

wrong way   right way

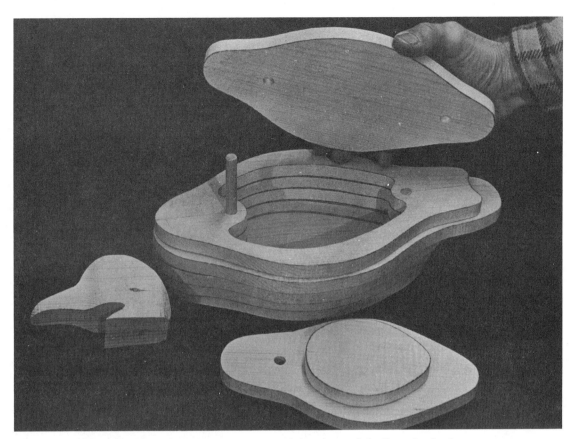

Illus. 54. The assembly of the layers on a stack laminated, hollow-body decoy.

Illus. 55. The glued-up assembly ready for final shaping. If left as is, wouldn't this make an interesting decoration?

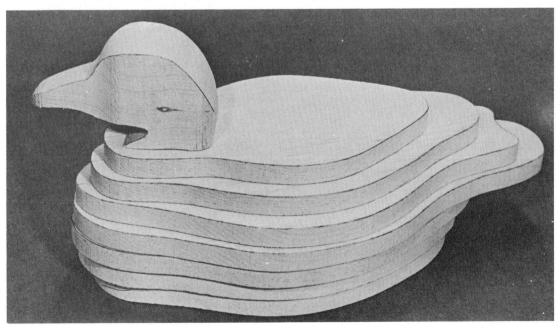

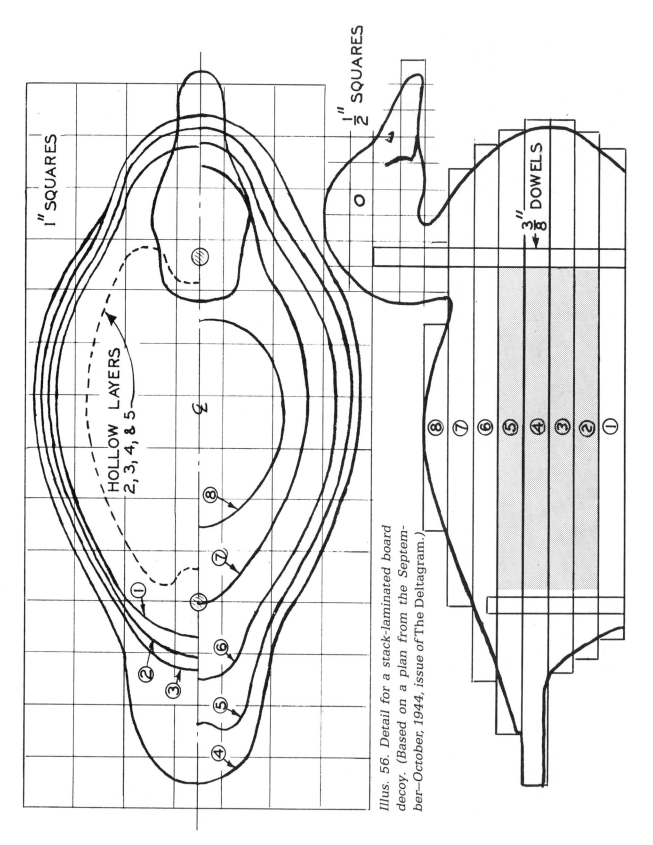

Illus. 56. Detail for a stack-laminated board decoy. (Based on a plan from the September–October, 1944, issue of The Deltagram.)

1" SQUARES

1½" SQUARES

3/8" DOWELS

HOLLOW LAYERS 2, 3, 4, & 5

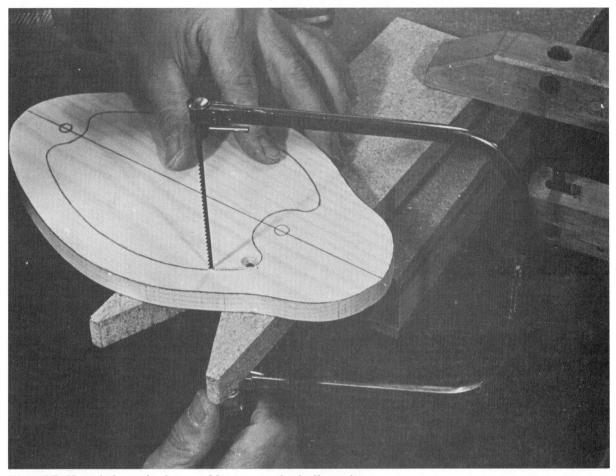

Illus. 57. Here is how the internal layers can be hollowed out.

thin, presawn boards. The drawing, illustration 56, gives all the details. Hollow out four layers with a coping saw, as shown in illustration 57. This is an excellent method if you have limited access to power tools. This decoy, when finally shaped could be given a natural or stained finish, but because of its many glue lines it would probably be best to paint it.

Illus. 58. A roughed-out solid-body decoy cut entirely with a bandsaw.

Illus. 59. Two solid blocks laid out, ready for the initial cutting.

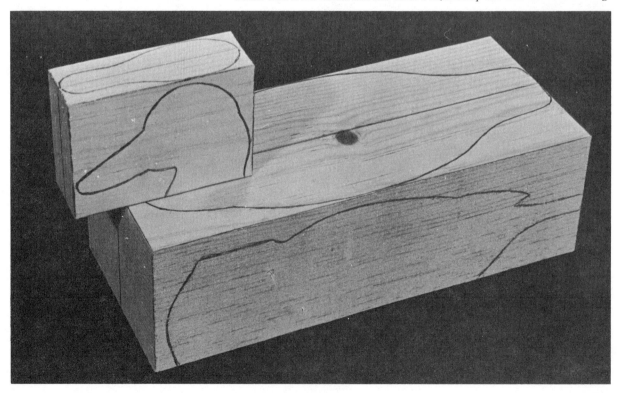

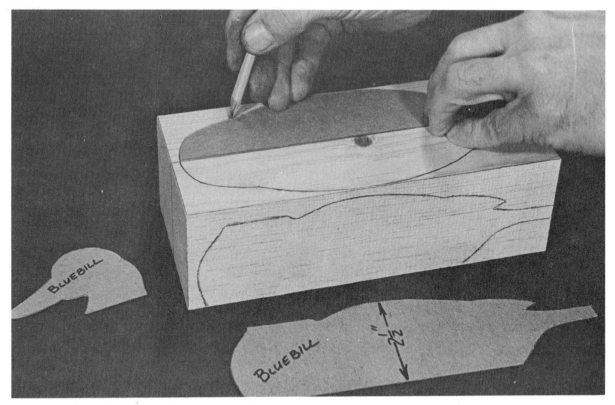

Illus. 60. Making the top-view layout with a half-template pattern.

SOLID, ONE-PIECE BODY (See illustration 58.) This is the easiest and fastest type of construction, providing (1) you have access to a bandsaw, or (2) you will be making a less-than-lifesize decoy, and/or (3) you have good, dry wood of the proper size.

Begin with a block slightly larger than you need, to accommodate the thickness, width, and length required. (See illustration 59.) Make templates of paper or cardboard, to transfer the lines from the plan to the wood as shown in illustration 60. Note that the shapes are laid out on two surfaces—the edge and top surfaces of the block. The top view, which is usually symmetrical, is laid out on a lengthwise center line with a half template.

Saw out the side view or edge profile with a bandsaw, as shown in illustrations 61 and 62. If you don't have the use of a bandsaw, this job can be done with a sharp, wide carpenter's chisel. Once the block has been sawn to its side-view profile shape, nail the waste pieces back on (illustration 63) and cut the top-view shape on the bandsaw, as shown in illustrations 64 and 65. If no bandsaw is available, this job can be done by hand with a chisel, as shown in illustration 66.

Now cut off the corners using a chisel, draw knife, or with the bandsaw, as shown in illustrations 67 and 68.

Illus. 61. Sawing out the side-view shape.

Illus. 62. The side-view cut completed.

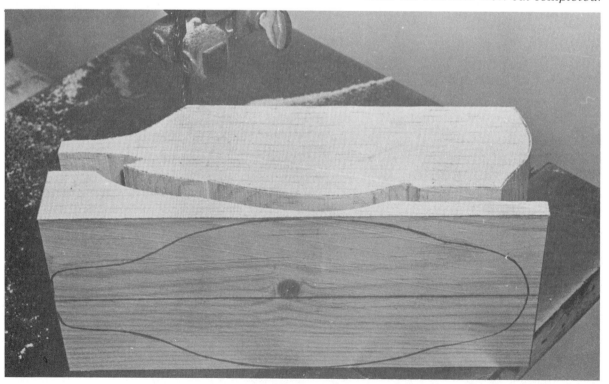

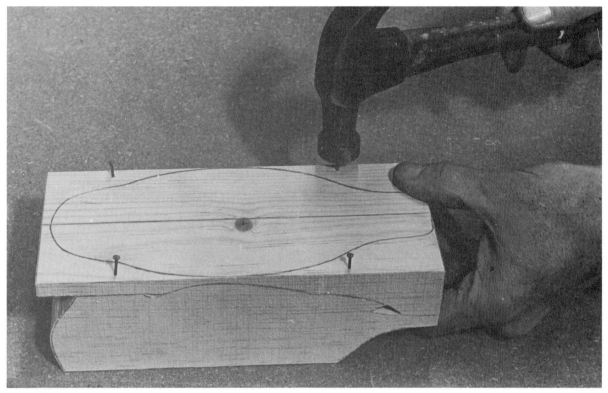

Illus. 63. Reattaching the waste piece so the top view can be cut.

Illus. 64. Making the top-view cut.

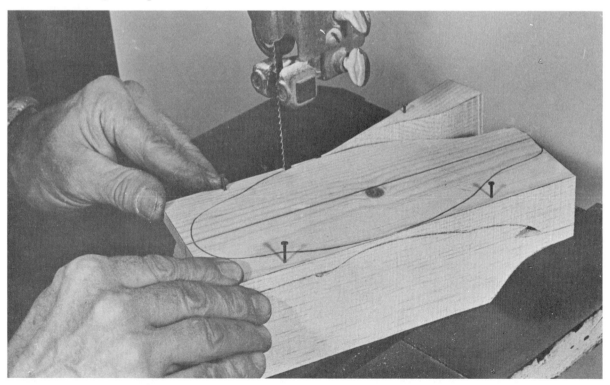

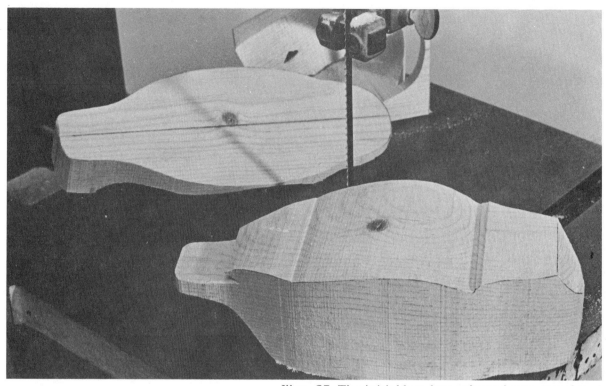

Illus. 65. The initial bandsaw-shaped cuts completed.

Illus. 66. Chiselling the top.

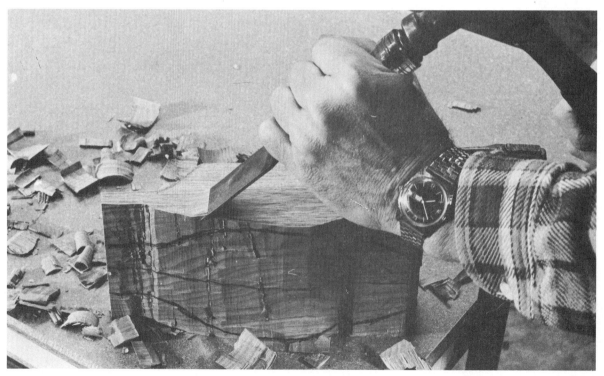

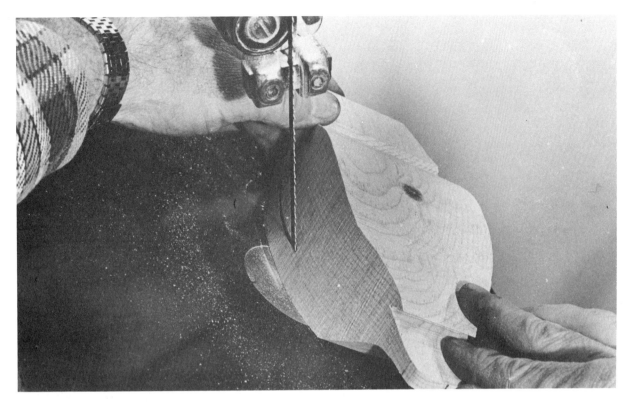

Illus. 67. Using the bandsaw with the table tilted to "knock off" the corners.

Illus. 68. Another view of the bandsaw being used to bring the decoy closer to the intended shape.

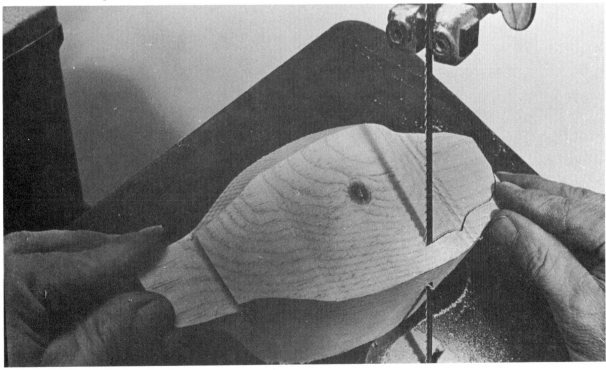

Illus. 69. A rough-sawn 2-inch (5-cm) plank being face-jointed and levelled on the jointer.

TWO-PIECE HOLLOW CONSTRUCTION This is a practical method for most full-sized decoys, provided you can obtain planks of suitable thickness. This method usually requires only one glue line in the body, and it is often located so it is of minimal visibility. If your wood is good and dry and if you intend to make a decorative decoy, hollowing each piece will reduce internal stress of the wood and minimize the possibility of future cracking. Prepare the pieces as you would for any good glue joint. The surfaces should be smooth and flat. Face the pieces on a jointer (illustration 69), or carefully flatten them with a sharp hand plane.

Hold the two pieces together and lay out the side view profile and top view shape on the appropriate surfaces. (See illustration 70.) Determine the best location for two wood screws to be driven in (from the bottom) to hold both pieces together. Screw the two pieces together. (See illustration 71.)

The decoy body is now worked to rough shape with a bandsaw or by hand, as previously described and illustrated. Further shaping and rounding of the body should be done, bringing it as close as possible to its finished, contoured shape before removing the screws. Separate the pieces and hollow out the inside. Use a hand drill, a power hand drill, or the drill press to remove excessive material by boring overlapping holes. (See illustrations 72 and 73.) A chisel and/or gouge can also be used for this job. Glue the halves together.

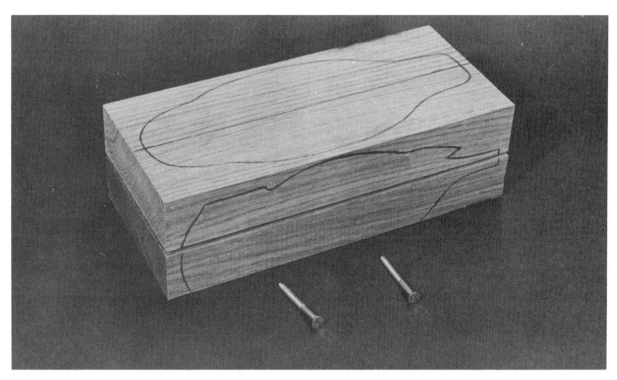

Illus. 70. The two pieces are laid out before being fastened together with wood screws.

Illus. 71. The two halves fit tightly together. Note that the joint is hardly visible.

Illus. 72. A forstner bit in the drill press works well for hollowing out the inside surfaces of each piece.

Illus. 73. The assembly of the hollowed-out halves. It is a good idea to insert a small steel nut or similar item so it rattles around the inside. This tells others that you have hollowed out the body.

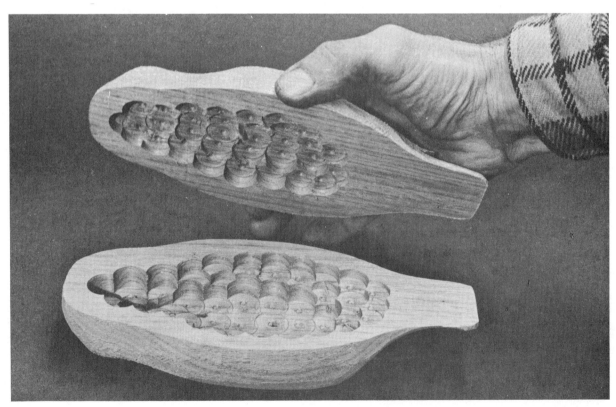

Illus. 74. (Above) Laying out the side view of the head.

Illus. 75. Drilling the eye sockets.

Illus. 76. Drilling for the dowel joint.

ROUGHING OUT THE HEADS
(See illustrations 74–78.) Saw out the profile shape of the head using a coping saw, jigsaw, or bandsaw. (See illustration 74.) Be sure the grain runs lengthwise in line with the bill. Some carvers do as much work as possible to the head before gluing it to the body. This includes drilling out the eyes (illustration 75), which assures they will be perfectly aligned. To be sure the hole is exactly the right size for the glass eye make a test hole in a piece of scrap. Drilling the dowel joint (illustration 76) is a good idea while the block is still in its rectangular shape with

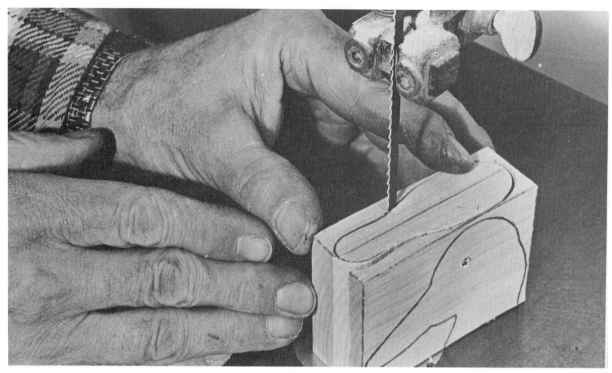

Illus. 77. If a top-view cut is to be made, it's easier to do it before cutting out the side view.

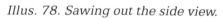
Illus. 78. Sawing out the side view.

squared, parallel surfaces. Drill a $^{17}/_{64}''$ (6.7 mm) diameter hole for a $\frac{1}{4}''$ (6.35 mm) dowel. If desired, the top-view shape of the head and bill contour can be cut (illustration 77) before sawing out the side-view profile shape (illustration 78).

It may be necessary to level and smooth the gluing area (for the head) on the body to effect a good glue joint. This can be accomplished by hand, using a chisel to make a perfectly flat surface. An alternative method is to use a flat-bottom router bit in a drill press. (See illustration 79.) Be sure to feed the work against the rotation direction of the bit. Use the highest speed (RPM) possible.

Make a dry run assembly of the head to the body to assure that a good clean joint will result. Now, glue the head to the body. If you use a quick-setting woodworking glue, you can press the head against the body by hand, holding it for a few minutes until the glue sets. To glue heads on working or painted decoys, I suggest five-minute epoxy glue. This glue has good gap-filling qualities, is ideal for less-than-perfect-fitting joints, and does not require pressure.

Illus. 79. Levelling and smoothing the gluing area of the body with a router bit installed in a drill press.

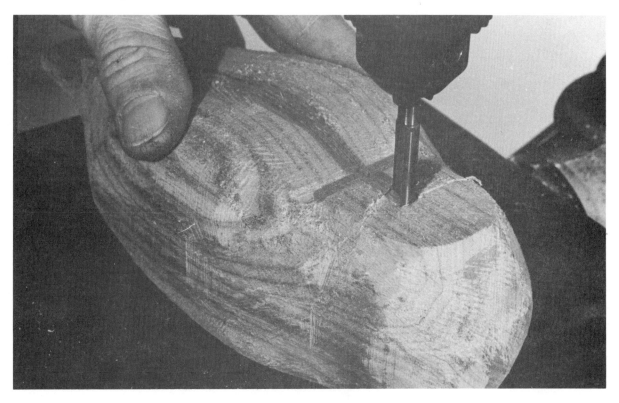

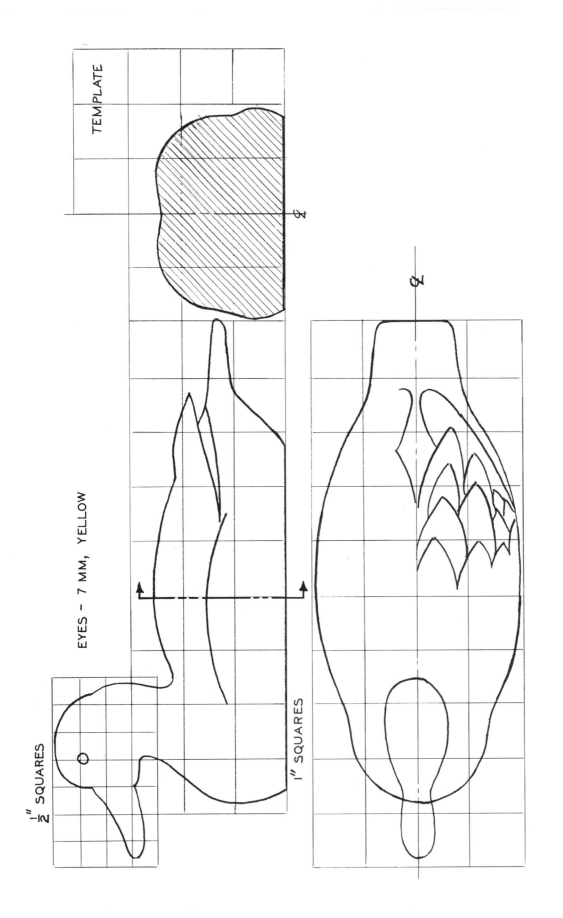

TEMPLATE

EYES – 7 MM, YELLOW

½" SQUARES

1" SQUARES

Illus. 80. The plan for a half-size bluebill (scaup) developed by Keith Bridenhagen.

5

Keith Bridenhagen Carves a Decoy

This chapter illustrates the decoy-carving techniques employed by Keith Bridenhagen, a well-known and productive artist from Sister Bay, Wisconsin. Keith demonstrates every step involved to make a simple decorative decoy. Starting with a crudely rough-sawn block, Keith shows how he works it through all the stages of carving and final contour shaping. Keith shows how to work a decoy to the point where it is ready for either a natural finish or a simple paint job, or ready to be worked further by adding feather texturing and additional realistic painting. Finishing, feather detailing, and painting are covered in the next two chapters.

Two remarkable qualities of Keith's work are his speed and the simplicity of his technique. The latter should prove to be a good confidence-builder for the beginner. Keith makes it look so easy, you say to yourself, ''I can do that!'' And, you can, once you give it a try.

The steps shown here are precisely the same as those Keith practices himself as he works in his own shop/gallery making decoys to sell. Many of his decoy designs and finished decoys are illustrated throughout this book. Keith also makes elaborately detailed realistic decoys, which he enters in various competitive carving contests throughout the United States.

You will be quick to observe that Keith's tools are very basic, but very effectively used. His limited tools are certainly adequate enough for him to turn out hundreds of decoys. In fact, Keith does not own a bandsaw. He borrows one to rough out his blocks. Another item that is not one of Keith's accessories, is a carving vise. Only occasionally, in the course of making a decoy, does he clamp the block to a workbench. Most of his work is performed in a sitting position, much like that of an old-time whittler. The workbench is more often his lap. His vise is one hand, holding the decoy against his leg or body, as he tools it with the other hand.

The decoy selected for this demonstration is a simple bluebill (scaup), of Keith's own design, in about one-half full size. (See the drawing, illustration 80, for details.) This is an excellent plan and carving for a beginner's first decoy.

Keith begins each of his decoy carvings with the head already dowelled and glued to the body. The wood he will use for this decoy is straight-grained white cedar. The forty-seven illustrations that follow tell the story in complete step-by-step progression. Refer to Chapter Seven to see how this little decoy can be further detailed with feather texturing and painting. Read on!

Illus. 81. The simple rough-sawn block Keith starts with. Clamped to a bench, Keith "knocks off" the corners of the upper body with a chisel, working with the grain. Note that the center line must be redrawn (lengthwise along the body) after sawing out the blank.

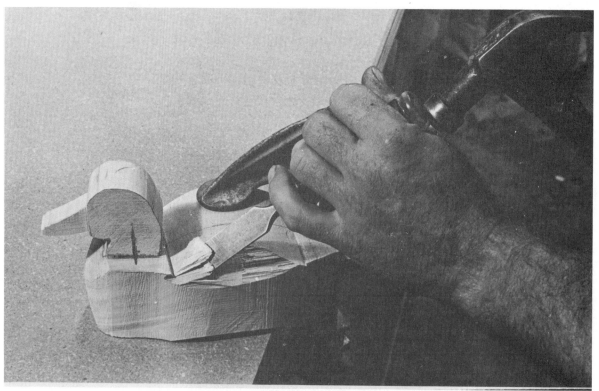

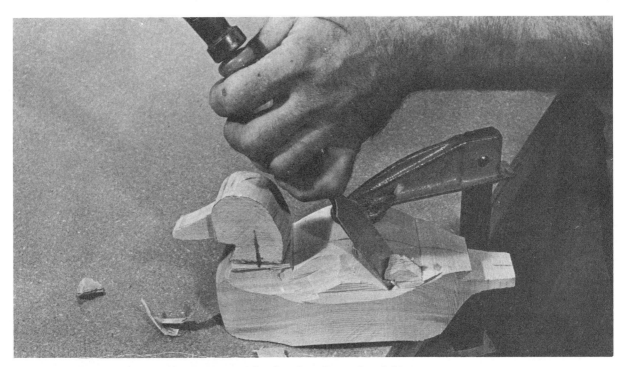

Illus. 82. The chisel is used to remove big chunks of wood quickly.

Illus. 83. Chisel marks are removed with a small half-round rasp. Notice that the center-line area is not worked.

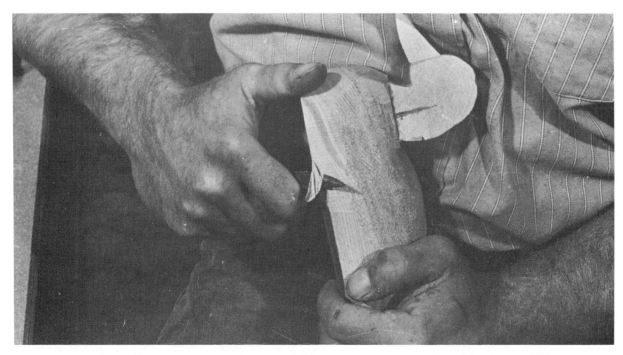

Illus. 84. With a knife, Keith rounds the bottom edges, again working with the grain, as in whittling.

Illus. 85. A coping saw is used to remove difficult "end grain" corners, which are cut more easily and faster with a coping saw than a knife.

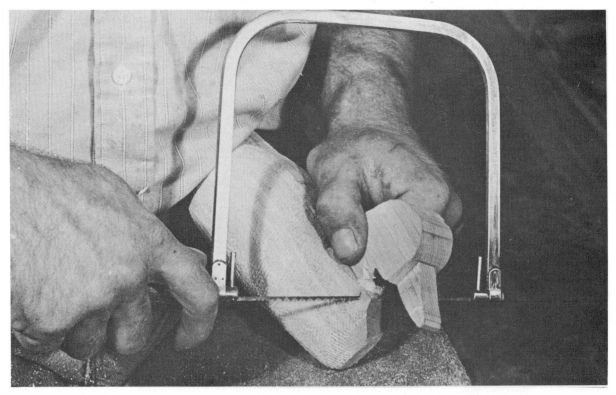

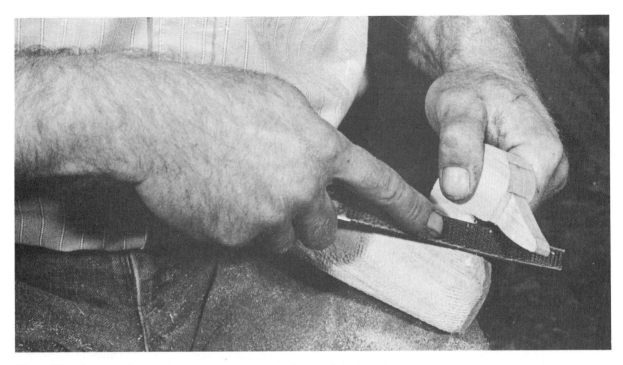

Illus. 86. The rasp is again used to round the front of the body.

Illus. 87. The coping saw removes the corners of the body under the tail.

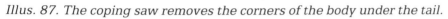

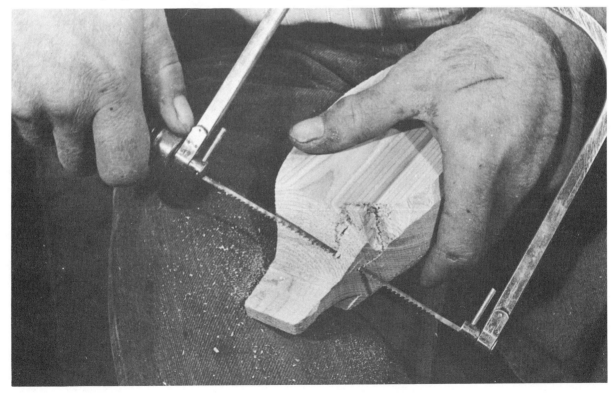

Illus. 88. Shape the under-tail with a knife. Slice with the grain to remove chips.

Illus. 89. The rear and under-tail are smoothed out with the same small half-round rasp.

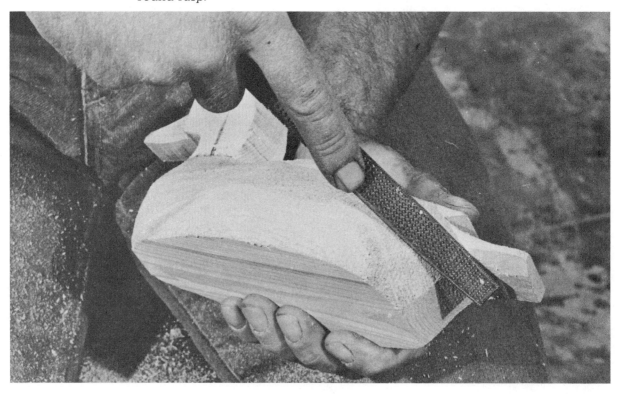

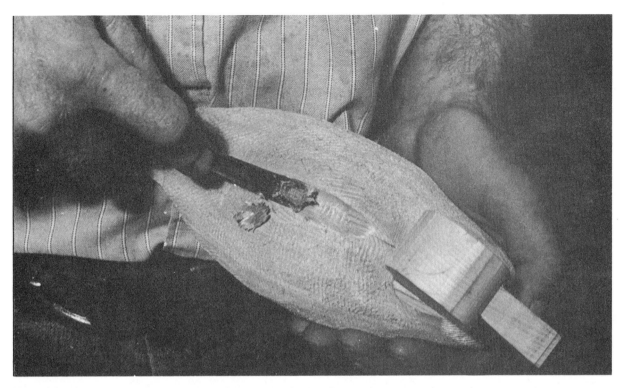

Illus. 90. Here Keith cuts a depression along the back, cutting away the center line with a small, but very sharp gouge.

Illus. 91. The knife is used to round over the sharp edges left by the gouge.

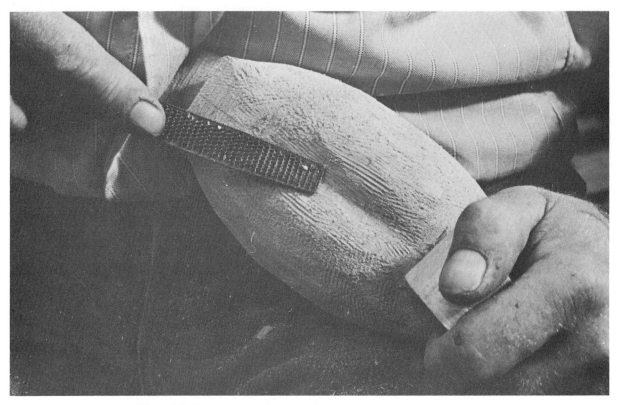

Illus. 92. Once again the small half-round rasp is put to use, to even out the knife marks.

Illus. 93. (Opposite) With the body essentially shaped, Keith "eyeballs" it to check for symmetry. A pencil marks areas needing further removal.

Illus. 94. After 12 to 15 minutes of work Keith's decoy reaches this point of completion.

Illus. 95. The first step to working the head is drawing a center line over the top and back, as shown.

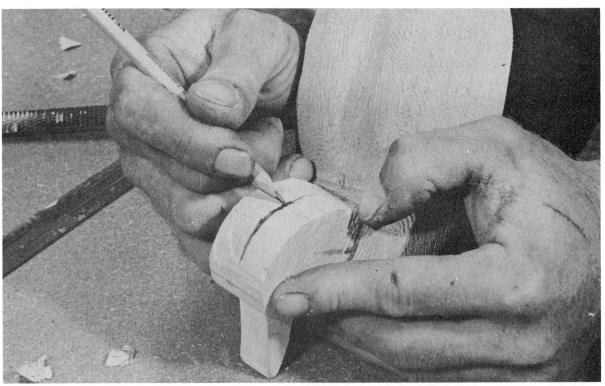

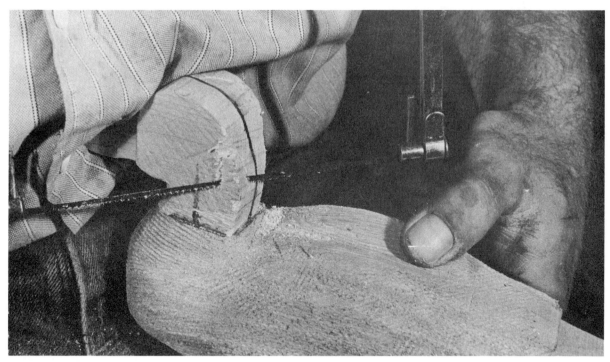

Illus. 96. The coping saw is drawn into use to remove the corners at the rear-neck area, cutting down to the body.

Illus. 97. The width of the upper-head area is reduced using the carving knife.

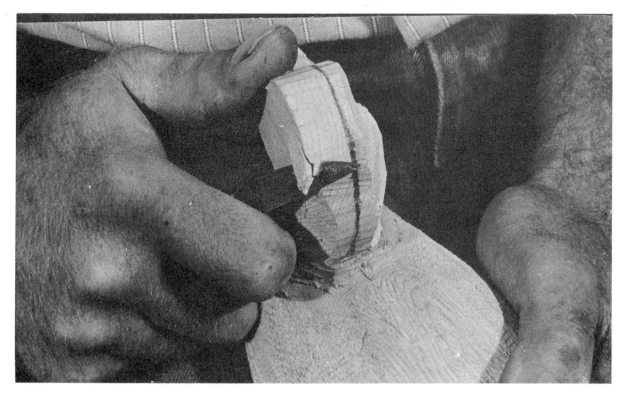

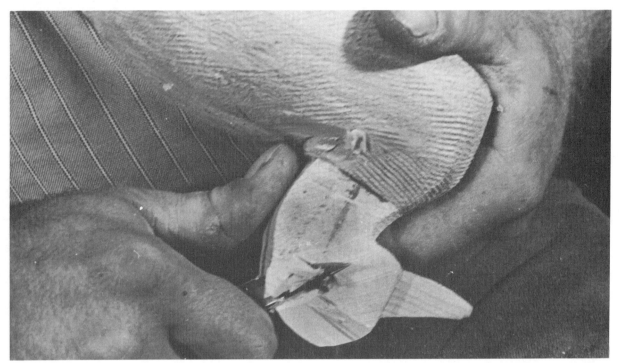

Illus. 98. Keith uses a knife on the back of the head to round over the corners made by the coping saw.

Illus. 99. Here the coping saw cuts away the front of the neck and takes off the corners towards the bill.

Illus. 100. Now the knife is used to shape up towards the bill.

Illus. 101. The head is carved toward the bill, simultaneously giving shape to the cheeks.

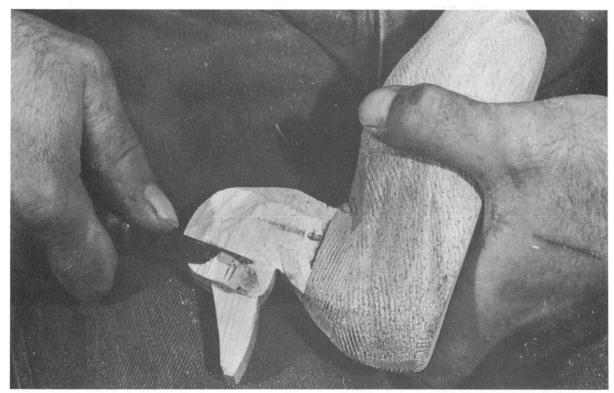

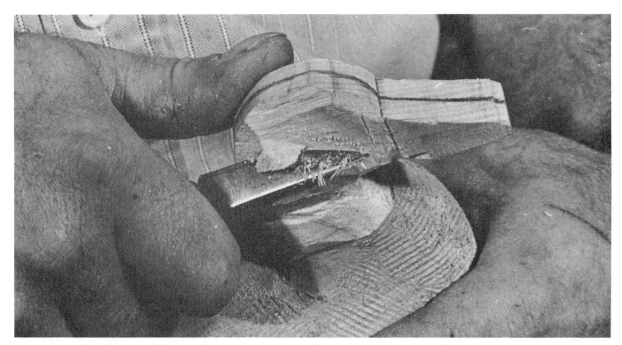

Illus. 102. With a cross-grain cutting-action, the knife is used to scoop out the eye area and give more form to the cheeks.

Illus. 103. Knife work continues from the top of the head towards the bill.

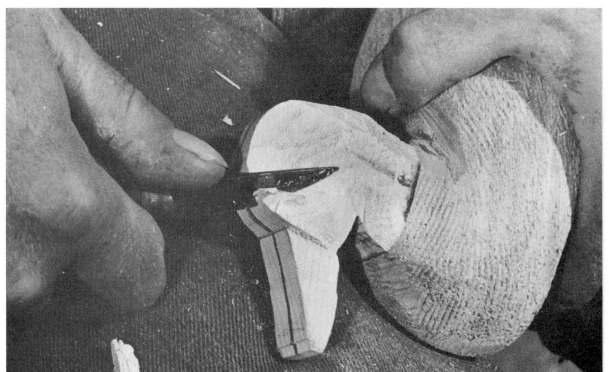

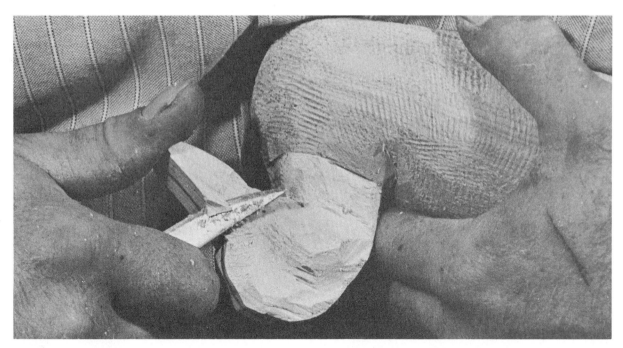

Illus. 104. The upper bill is rounded over. Note that Keith has maintained the original center line.

Illus. 105. The head roughed out. Not too pretty at this point, but look on.

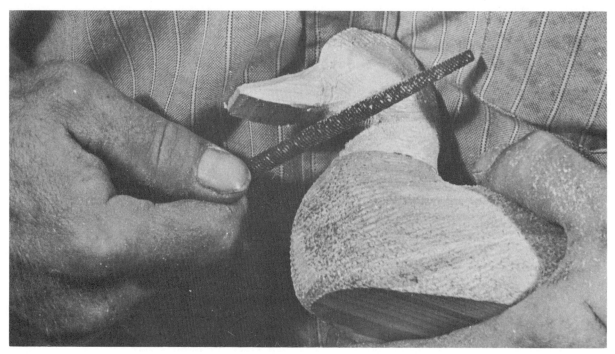

Illus. 106. A small round rasp rounds out the front-neck area.

Illus. 107. Keith files the rear neck, shaping it into the body. An important observation at this point: Keith uses the rasp only to smooth out coping-saw cuts and knife cuts, not to remove huge amounts of wood.

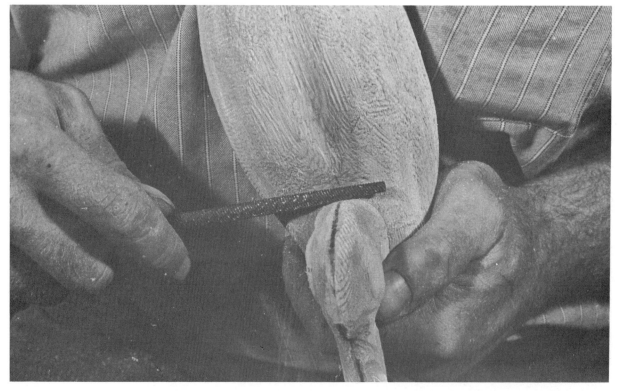

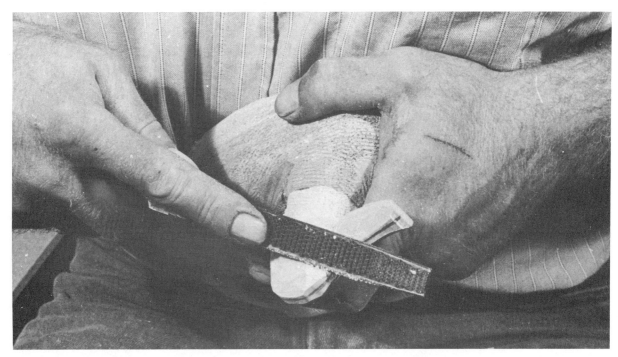

Illus. 108. The half-round rasp is again put to use, here to smooth out the cheek-to-upper-bill contours.

Illus. 109. The knife is used to delicately finish-carve the bill. Upon completion, the decoy could be sanded and finished if no further details are desired.

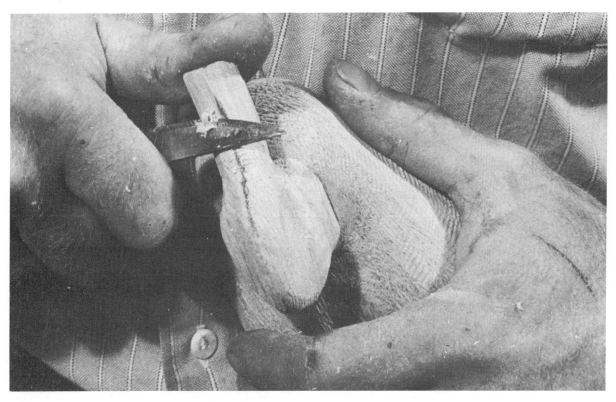

Illus. 110. The work now begins for carving the primary feathers. First a center line is drawn down the rear back. Then a diamondlike pattern is laid out as shown here (and on the drawing plan, illus. 80).

Illus. 111. The wing primaries are laid out freehand by extending lines from the tail to form a long, sharp V cut, as shown.

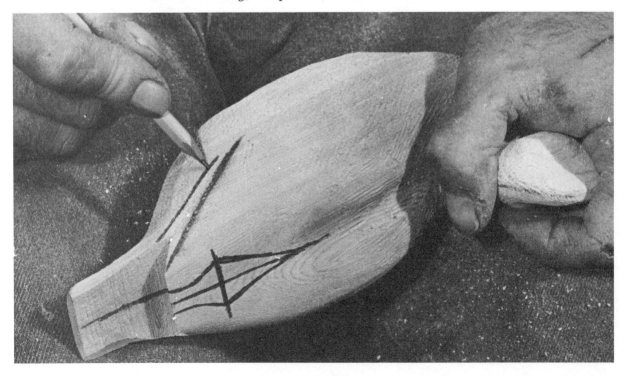

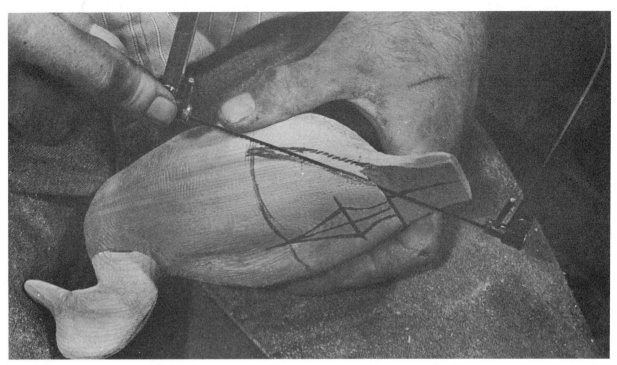

Illus. 112. Making the first cut of a narrow V cut under the wing.

Illus. 113. The second cut removes the V-shaped piece. Naturally, these cuts are made to both sides of the body.

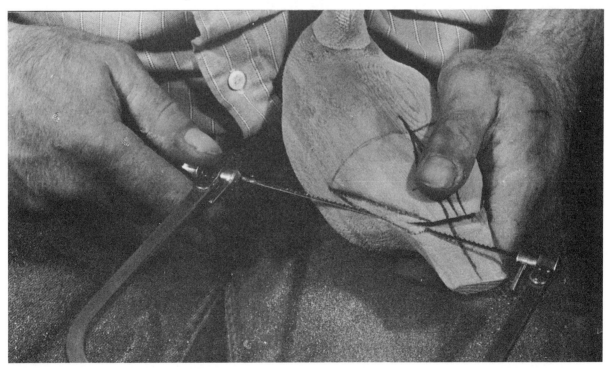

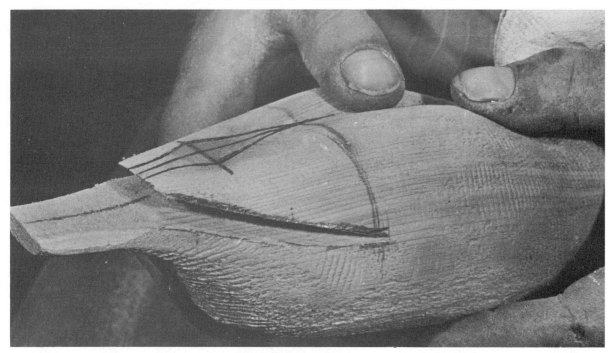

Illus. 114. Here is the result.

Illus. 115. The diamondlike separation between the primaries is cut out, tapering to a depth equal to the top of the tail. Here the work is clamped, to free both hands for better control of the power-driven rotary cutter.

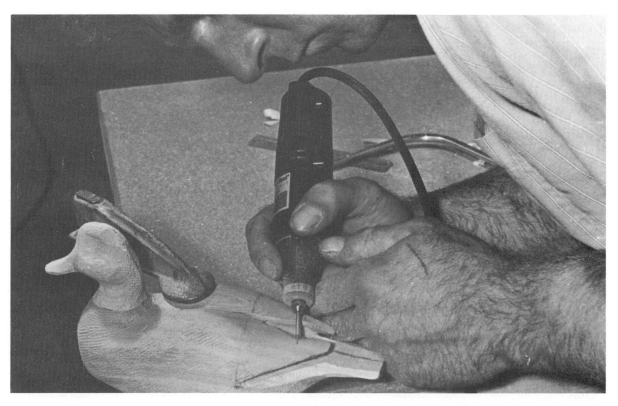

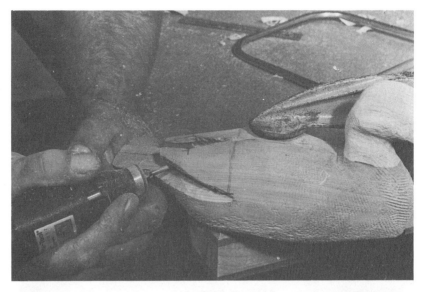

Illus. 116. Keith again uses the Dremel Power Tool to further cut and smooth under the primaries.

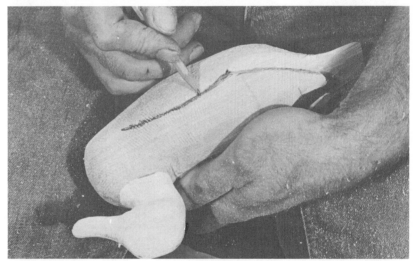

Illus. 117. With the primaries and wingtips shaped, Keith now draws a line toward the front for the side flank.

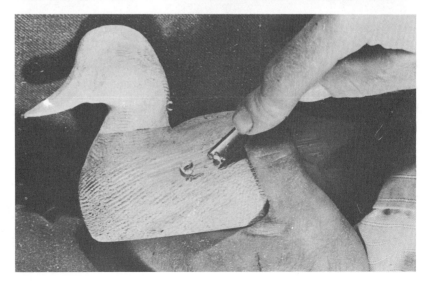

Illus. 118. The small gouge is used to cut a shallow groove along the flank line on each side of the body.

Illus. 119. (Left) A final check can be made with a template as shown. However, with Keith's experience this template is not really needed.

Illus. 120. (Below) Here's what it looks like so far. Once again, at this point the decoy can be sanded and finished, or more work can be done on it.

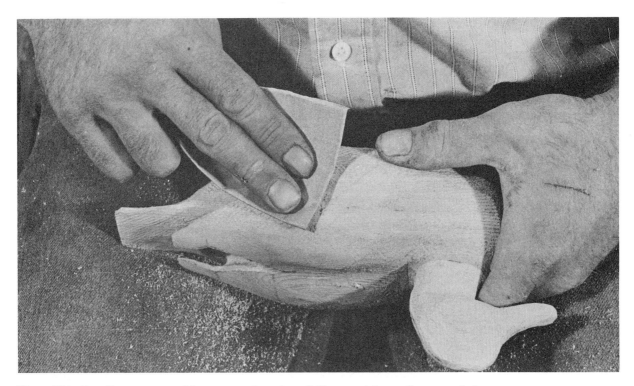

Illus. 121. Sanding starts with coarse abrasive, follows with medium, and then finishes with fine when all the tool marks are removed.

Illus. 122. Looking directly over the head and marking the vertical location of the eves.

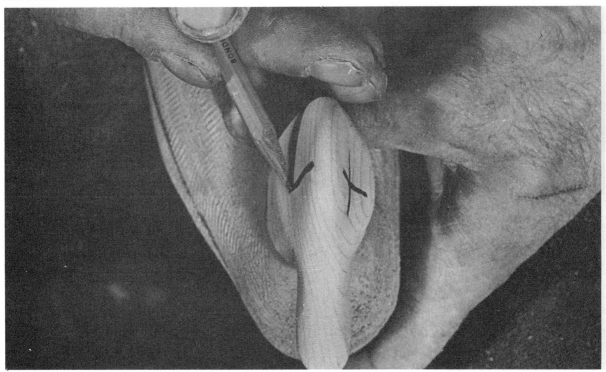

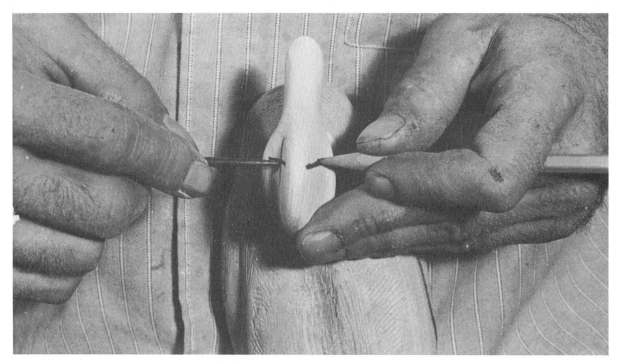

Illus. 123. A scratch awl helps pinpoint alignment of the second eye.

Illus. 124. The holes for the glass eyes are drilled carefully.

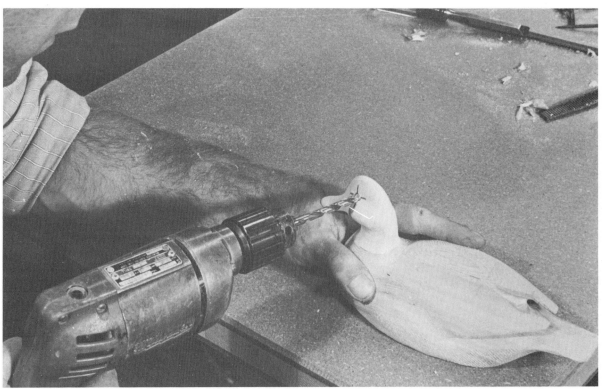

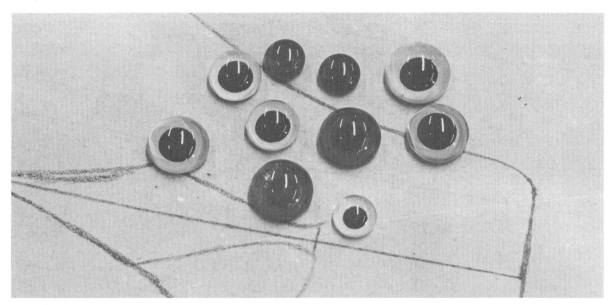

Illus. 125. A close-up of glass eyes in various sizes and colors. Refer to page 121 for a chart giving sizes and colors of eyes to use for various kinds of other decoys.

Illus. 126. The eyes are held in place by ordinary wood filler. First put some filler into the hole, working it in and around the sides of the hole. Use a filler that will match the final finish tone if the decoy will have a stained or natural finish. Any color filler can be used if the decoy is to be painted.

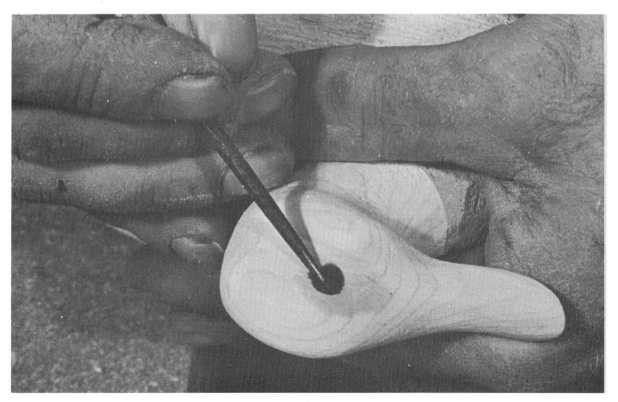

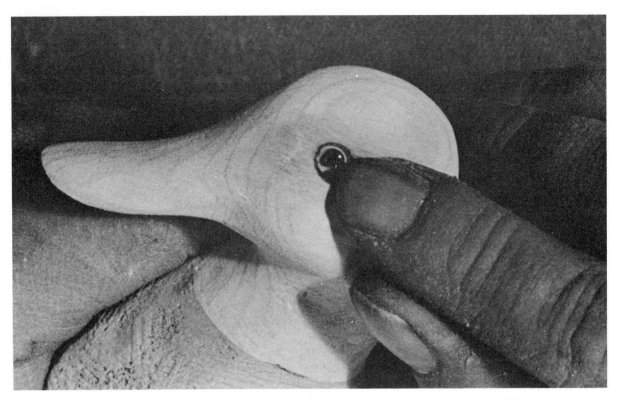

Illus. 127. With the head sanded, press the eye into the fresh filler to a proper-looking depth, firmly seating the eye. Remove filler-squeeze-out carefully with a sharp knife. Again, at this point the decoy can be finished, or some basic feather texture details can be added. See Chapter 6.

6

The Natural Wood Finish

If your decoy is fashioned from any of the woods exhibiting beautiful figure (graining) you will likely want to enrich its appearance with a stained or clear natural finish. Although there are those who like the unfinished look, some sort of top coat is recommended to seal and protect the wood, since people will want to handle and admire your decoy.

Any of the conventional wood-finishing systems of stains, sealers, and clear top coats of varnishes, lacquers, oil resins, and so on can be used to finish your decoy. Just do it as you would finish any other woodworking project. If you elect to stain, remember that end grains will suck up more stain and turn out darker than other areas. Since you have invested a considerable effort in your decoy up to this point, you want to be absolutely sure you will get the final look you want. Consequently, be sure to use a quality-brand finishing system, and, most importantly, test it first on a scrap of the same kind of wood.

If you are into decoy work, it is most probable that you are already experienced in woodworking and have sufficient knowledge about the basics of wood finishing. If not, confer with your local supplier of finishing materials or refer to a general woodworking book for this information.

Remember, the execution of a well-finished block, one that represents your finest workmanship, hinges a great deal on good sanding. (See illustration 128.) Careful attention to dent and scratch removal is most important, particularly if you are staining your decoy or using a high-gloss top coat. These two materials tend to call attention to careless sanding jobs.

If any cracks, checks, pitch pockets, wormholes, nail holes, or other kinds of holes are visible in the surface, they can be filled. I think that fillers draw attention to themselves. They interfere with the natural flow of the lines and color tones of the wood itself. Seldom do even the most experienced wood finishers make a perfect, inconspicuous match or cover-up. I think filling such areas is somewhat the admission of a mistake, of poor planning, or of poor workmanship. The decoyist is attempting to hide and conceal from the viewer the naturalness of the wood. On the other hand, if such defects in your block are significantly large, conspicuous, and to your total disliking, you can always fill the voids and paint the decoy. (Refer to pages 109–120 for information about painting decoys.)

SIGNING YOUR WORK (See illustration 129.) It depends just exactly when the best time is to affix your mark or signature and date to the bottom of the decoy. I think it is best to do it on the raw wood, if possible, under the finish. The only problem is that your signature or mark may be dissolved by some finishes. Signatures can be made with a ball-point pen, or fine waterproof soft-tip pen with India ink. They can also be painted, branded, or whatever. Test the finish over your mark on a scrap piece of wood. Obviously, if your decoy is to be painted, signing would be the last thing to do. In such case, pen and India ink, a custom brand, or printed sticker can suffice.

Illus. 128. Thorough sanding with fine-grit abrasive is essential.

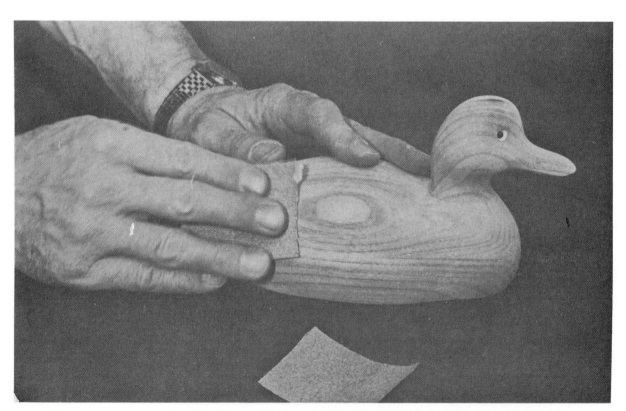

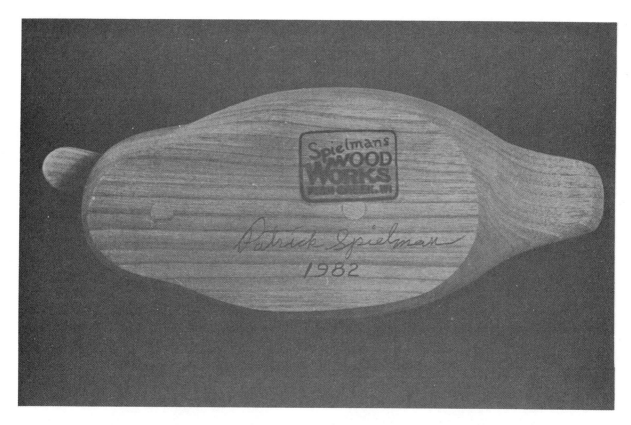

Illus. 129. Sign your work, using a pen, branding iron, sticker, or other distinctive mark.

It is essential that you do put your own identifying mark or signature on every decoy you make. It adds to the individuality, character, and value of the decoy. Further, it certainly indicates that the decoy is handmade and a one-of-a-kind work of art. Real working decoys of days long past were always marked or branded. This was done more to identify the owner rather than the maker, because decoys were often loaned, stolen, or lost.

Illustrations 130, 131, and 132 show some popular, easy to apply finishes. There are literally hundreds of different stains and kinds of natural finishes available. Just be sure to read all label instructions and the manufacturer's safety precautions for any new or unfamiliar finishing material. Also, in such cases make a test run on a sample of the same wood, to be assured of getting the look, color, feel, and sheen you really want.

Illus. 130. Danish oil finishes are very easy to apply and give the wood a soft, low lustre, hand-rubbed look.

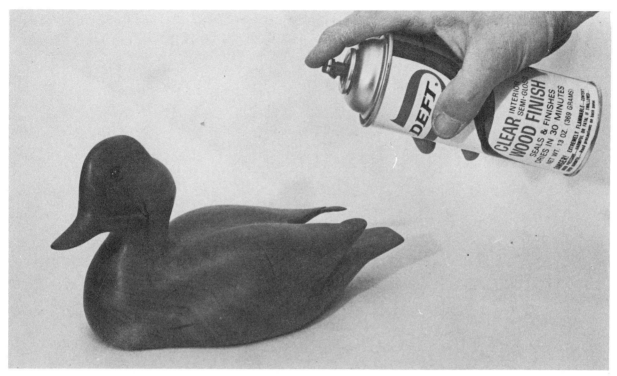

Illus. 131. Spraying with an aerosol is fast and easy. Here a solid cherry bufflehead gets a clear, fast-drying finish.

Illus. 132. This green-wing teal drake in wormy butternut is given a natural brush-on finish.

Illus. 133. Just a little carved feathering detail, as shown here on the primaries and tail, adds considerable interest to this natural-finished butternut loon made by Harold Schopf.

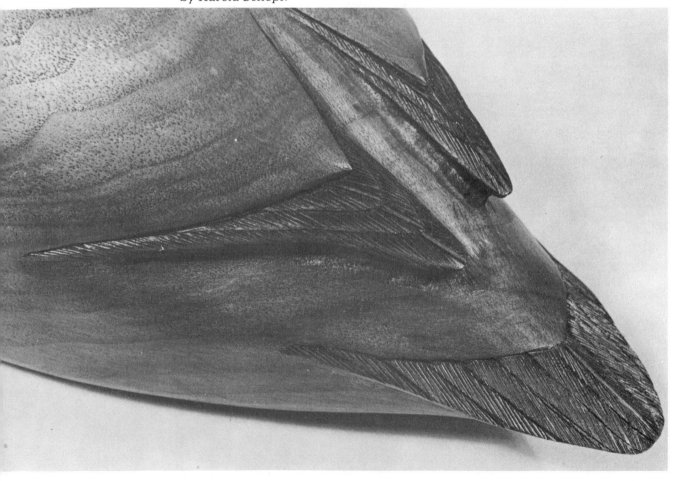

7

Basic Detailing and Painting

This chapter introduces the fundamentals necessary for adding some realistic details to your decoys. The content here is by no means all-inclusive, nor is it intended to be regarded as the authoritative approach to the subject. The information presented *will* guide you along as you progress beyond the level of making the basic, simple decoy. (See illustration 133.) This chapter is for those who have the patience and desire to become involved in a creative expression leading toward more realism in their decoys. When you at first look at a detailed decorative decoy (illustrations 134, 135, and 136) with the thought of doing it yourself, it's almost frightening. However, as in any craft of significance there are often techniques of surprising simplicity when the job is analyzed and taken step by step. There are as many different ideas how and ways to get the job done as there are different decoy makers. This chapter will show how Keith Bridenhagen does it.

However, before starting, familiarize yourself with some of the duck's anatomy. (See illustration 137.) Having an understanding of the bird's basic parts is fundamental to the procedures involved to simulate the duck's varied textured surfaces. Being somewhat familiar with the basic characteristics of various waterfowl species is also essential. Seek out books on the identification and classification of birds and waterfowl. One good basic resource book is *The Key to North American Waterfowl* by Wylie and Furlong. Audubon books, field guides, preserved or actual specimens will be of major assistance in creating realistic details.

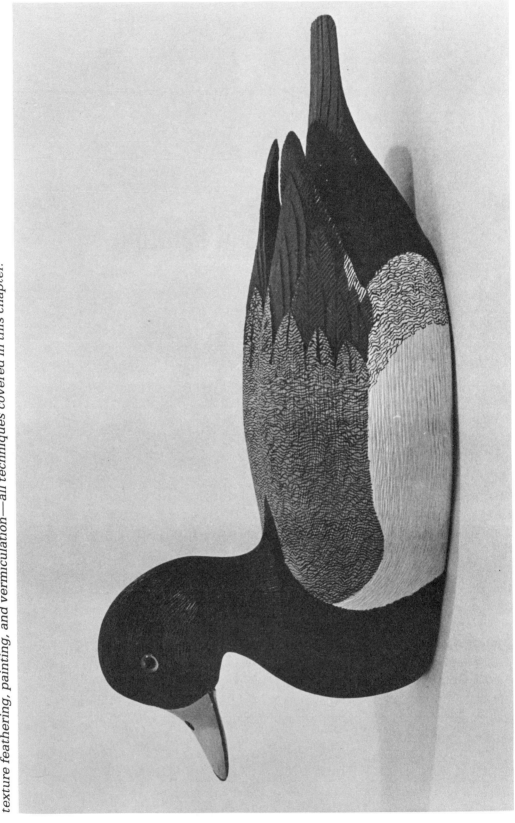

Illus. 134. Here is Keith Bridenhagen's bluebill (scaup) from Chapter 5, completely finished with some carved texture feathering, painting, and vermiculation—all techniques covered in this chapter.

Illus. 135. A close-up of feather texturing and painted vermiculation details.

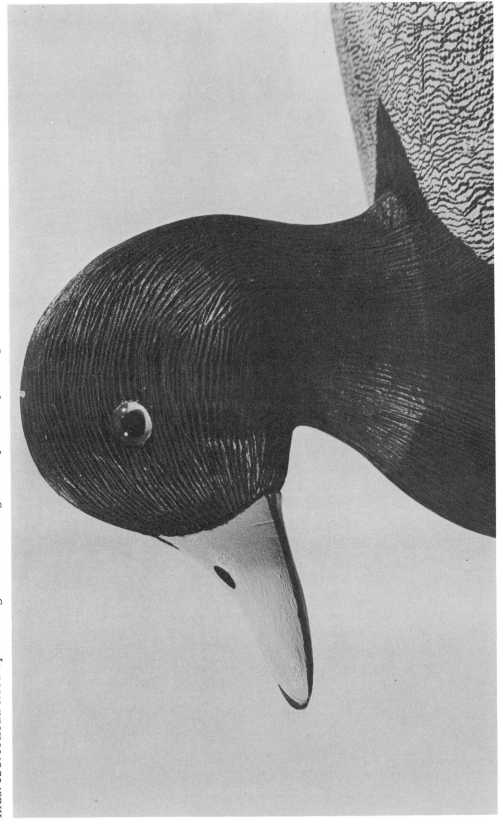

Illus. 136. A head close-up showing other texturing techniques and painting detail on Keith Bridenhagen's bluebill.

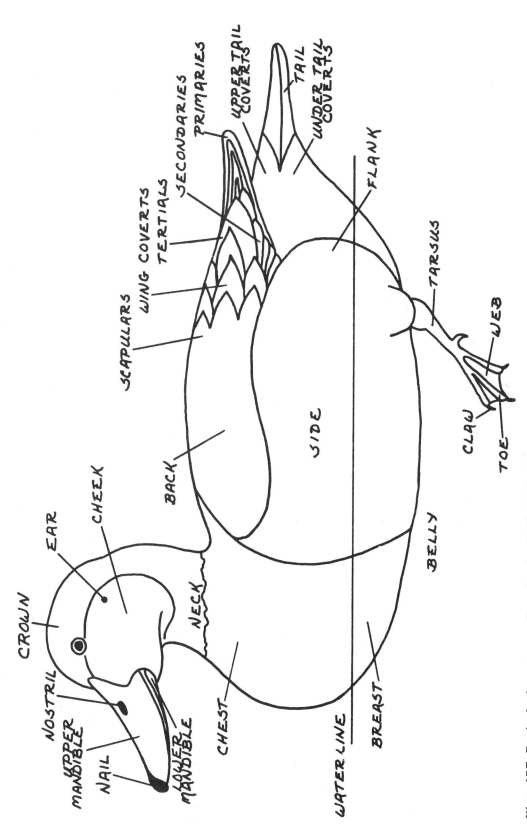

CROWN

EAR

CHEEK

NOSTRIL

UPPER MANDIBLE

NAIL

LOWER MANDIBLE

CHEST

NECK

BACK

SCAPULARS

WING COVERTS

TERTIALS

SECONDARIES

PRIMARIES

UPPER TAIL COVERTS

TAIL

UNDER TAIL COVERTS

FLANK

TARSUS

WEB

CLAW

TOE

SIDE

BELLY

BREAST

WATER LINE

Illus. 137. Basic duck anatomy. Drawing by Keith Bridenhagen.

In general ducks are categorized into two basic groups: puddle ducks and diving ducks.

PUDDLE DUCKS These are also referred to as marsh or pond ducks. They are primarily surface-feeding, and are generally identified by their up-turned tail and narrower beam (body width). The male and female are often of different plumage (feathering and coloring). They usually have a brightly colored rectangular patch at the rear edge of each wing. The mallard is the best-known puddle duck in this classification, and, in fact, it is the most popular of all the ducks in the United States and the world over. Its strong reputation and popularity survived for centuries as it is not only a beautiful bird but an exceptionally sought-after game bird due to its excellent taste. Other puddle ducks that are popular as decoys include the black duck, the pintail, the widgeon, the green-wing teal, the wood duck, the shoveller, the gadwall and the ruddy duck.

DIVING DUCKS These are also called bay ducks. They are heavier, have a wider beam, and dive from the surface for food. They are generally identified by their lower down-turned tails. Popular diving ducks often worked into decoys include scaups (bluebills), canvasbacks, ring-necked ducks, redheads, golden eyes, old squaws, and loons. (A loon is not a duck. It's a bird and therefore not closely related to other species.)

MERGANSERS AND THE CANADIAN GOOSE These are also popular as decoys. They are categorized differently from other diving ducks in most field guides. Mergansers were not widely made into working decoys because they were rarely hunted due to the poor, fishy taste. However, they make beautiful decorative decoys. The Canadian goose feeds mostly on grass, corn, and grain fields near the water. Both sexes look alike, and they are easily identified by their long black necks and long heads with white cheeks.

In order to create a close simulation of a specific species duck, the block must first be as accurately proportioned as possible with regard to profile shape and other distinguishing characteristics in its form and contour. Check the drawings and plans in this chapter, or design your own based upon your research.

FEATHER DETAILING Even though the bird's surfaces will eventually be textured by carving or burning, it is best to sand the overall shape to smooth contours. Doing this will make feather layout easier. Carving or burning the feather texture will also be neater and cleaner with smooth starting surfaces. The drawing (illustration 138) shows the different kinds of feathering on a duck. Note that the chest and head areas are primarily short, linelike dashes. Other feathers have center shafts with barbs that radiate from the shaft.

CHEST AND BREAST

SECONDARY and TERTIAL

SHAFT

HEAD AND NECK

SIDE FEATHERS

TAIL FEATHERS

PRIMARIES

Illus. 138. Various special feather designs for carving and burning detail. Drawing by Keith Bridenhagen.

Illus. 139. On a Bridenhagen bluebill (as carved in Chapter 5), only the rear featuring will be texture carved. Here are the feather outlines as drawn freehand.

Transfer your planned feather designs, pencilling them onto the appropriate surfaces of the decoy. This is normally done freehand to one half the decoy. (See illustration 139.) At first, do not try to transfer every last feather in intimate detail. Just try to include enough feathers to give the impression of the correct anatomic detail, so the overall look is similar to the detailing plans shown on the drawings (illustrations 138 and 134–136.)

Draw each feather outline first. At first, forget the feather shaft and barb layout lines. Just draw out each overall feather shape, each in relative proportion, and at the appropriate location on the duck. Remember, this takes time so work patiently. Once you have half the decoy feathering laid out, repeat this pattern on the second side. This is fairly easy to repeat freehand. However, if you want exact duplication, trace the first half directly from the layout made on your decoy with thin tissue paper. Then with carbon paper and your pattern (flipped over) transfer the layout to the other half of your block. Now, finally, you are ready to go. (See illustration 139.)

Feather texturing can begin either by carving around the outline of each feather or by burning around each feather. Consider the carving method first. It is really not difficult. Carving gives realistic results and can be done easily with a sharp knife. (Illustrations 140–142 show how this is done.) Try

Illus. 140. Carve the feathers working from the front toward the tail. Here Keith outlines the first feather. Make a vertical, fibre-severing cut around the feather, following the line and cutting to a depth of about ¹⁄₁₆ inch (1.58 mm).

Illus. 141. Next, a somewhat horizontal slicing cut is made to lift out a chip. The objective is to create a slightly tapered surface extending from the next feather back towards the first, producing a layered look.

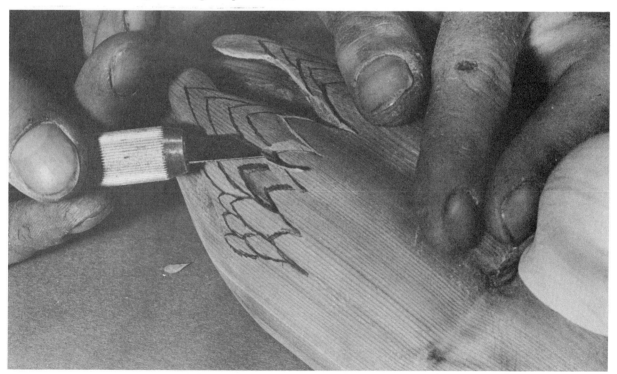

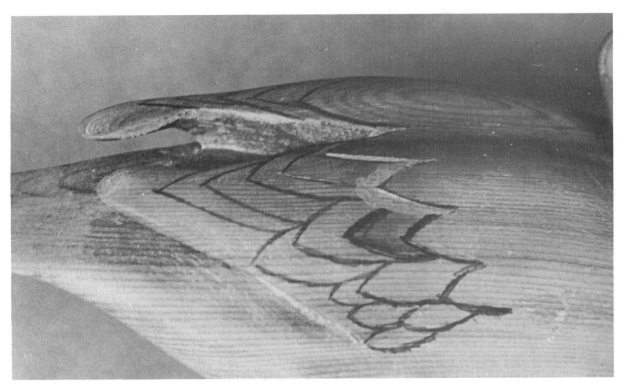

Illus. 142. A close-up view of a carved feather.

Illus. 143. Feather outlining and texturing with a burning tool.

to carve the feathers to a shingled layer or fish-scale-like effect, doing one feather at a time. This same technique can be done with a wood-burning tool as shown in illustration 143.

FEATHER-BURNING TOOLS These can be grouped into two categories. One category is comprised of tools intended for a variety of craft wood-burning jobs, including those in and out of the realm of bird feathering. (See illustration 144.) These tools come with some interchangeable tips suitable for shading as well as fine-line work. Essentially, this group is comprised of the heat-soldering, iron-type wood burners. The second group of wood

Illus. 144. An example of a teal hen feather-textured by burning. Note the interchangeable tips for the woodburning tool that can be used on this job.

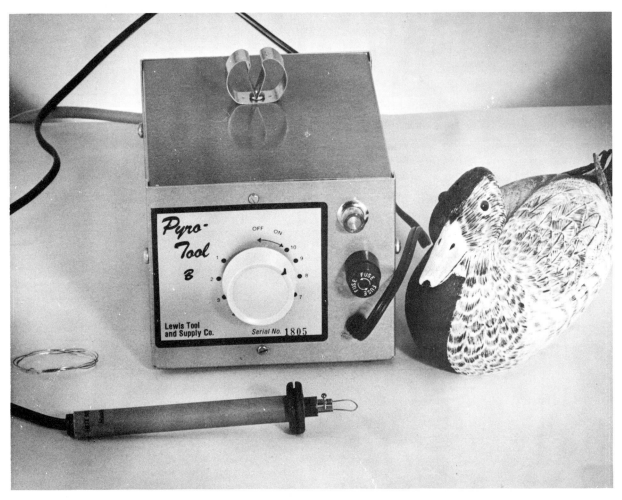

Illus. 145. The Pyro feather burner shown with a resistance-wire pen and rheostat control.

burners available, and the professional's choice, are those especially designed for burning lines on wood decoys to achieve realism. These have rheostats for controlling tip temperatures. There are other feather burners available incorporating fine Nichrome resistance wire tips (illustration 145) that you can flatten yourself for a very fine, knifelike edge. The best feather burners feature a rheostat control and have small lightweight pens with many interchangeable tip configurations available, allowing for more accuracy and more precise work.

On a practice piece, try using a burning tool with a bevelled skew tip to outline the individual feathers. Work the tool in such a manner to achieve the layered shingled or scaled look previously produced with a knife. Whichever method you're most comfortable with is the one to use.

FEATHER SHAFT AND BARBS If needed, with pencil draw in the shaft, dividing the feather in half. There is no need to draw in the barbs, unless you want a few lines to indicate their direction (as shown in illustration 138). Each feather can simulate actual texture by: (1) carving with a "v" carving tool, (2) using a miniature power tool with a suitable cutter, or (3) working with a wood burner. I think using a sharp wood-burning tool is the fastest and easiest of the three. However, when you try to burn in realistically barbs which should be very close to each other, you generally get an overall look of total charring. (See illustrations 146 and 147.) This is okay if the decoy is to

Illus. 146. After the shaft has been outlined, each individual barb is burned in by making successive incisions working from the shaft toward the outer edges. Here one half the feather is nearly completed.

Illus. 147. The completed feather made by feather-burned texturing.

be painted. However, if you intend to apply a clear or natural finish over your feathering detail, the burned barbs must be more cautiously done, leaving a space between each barb. Otherwise you can make the barb lines by careful hand carving or with the miniature power tool. Referring to the drawing, illustration 138, and the instructions that follow for burning the specific feather areas of the bird, should simplify the entire job for you.

BURNING IN THE PRIMARIES The primaries protrude out from under the tertial and secondary feathers. On some drawings they may appear as one feather, but they are not. These are a specific feather group and should be treated as such. Each feather has a shaft and its own individual barbs. Remember to burn the barbs by working from the shaft towards the outer edges.

SIDE, BACK, AND SCAPULAR FEATHERS The side feathers extend up to the chest and breast. They should be worked to appear as though they come from under the chest- and breast-area feathers. It is important that the feather shafts in these areas curve along the contour of the feathers.

TAIL, SECONDARY, AND TERTIAL FEATHERS Be sure the tail coverts lap over the tail feathers. Only the upper center feather of the tail section is completely exposed, with its shaft obviously visible. Refer again to illustration 138. The other tail feathers lap under the center feather and their shafts are not normally visible, unless the tail feathers are fanned out. In such a case, the other tail feathers become more totally visible, their feather shafts and barbs proportionally more visible. The secondary and tertial feathers are some of the largest on the carving and require great attention to detail. Remember to curve the shafts appropriately.

CHEST AND BREAST FEATHERS These are very small feathers extending downward from the neck area. They can also be lightly outline-carved if desired, to simulate a layered effect as on the other area feathers. Do not put shafts on these softer-looking feathers. Use short burning strokes in a fanlike pattern for each feather, as shown in illustration 138.

HEAD AND NECK FEATHERS These are very, very small microfeathers that are best simply simulated by a series of short-line incisions. Refer to illustrations 136 and 138. Each short line represents a hairlike feather and should follow the contour of the head, all flowing together where they meet other area feathers.

PAINTING There are many, many different possibilities for creating a painted duck. The ideas range from simple to complex, from dull to gaudy, and from a primitive look to a modern, stylized, totally unnatural one. Just to kick around a few ideas I've observed, I've seen beautiful, untextured decoys finished with antiquing—the same type of finish used to antique furniture. Kits for antiquing come in a wide range of color tones. They are available from most paint and hardware dealers. Perhaps you already have some in with your furniture-finishing supplies.

Illus. 148. Decoy-painting kits are available that provide the correct colors and "paint-by-numbers" instructions for many species.

A decoy painted entirely one color looks good; it can be covered with an earth tone for a subdued, decorator look. It could on the other hand, be painted a sparkling, flashy color with a bright high-gloss enamel or a metallic color to get lots of attention. I've also seen, believe it or not, decoys with painted flowers and some with transfer decals pasted to their backs. Tole-painted decoys and ones with *rosemaling* are also gaining in popularity. The ideas are almost limitless. Everyone has different taste and different ideas for expression.

For the most part, however, let's assume you want to follow the more conventional painting practice. The old decoy makers often overpainted their decoys, by emphasizing major features. They felt that if their decoys were more conspicuous than natural they would attract more birds.

Realistically painted decoys should pretty well match the duck's natural camouflaging colors of blue-green waters, muddy river banks, sea white-caps, and greens of the marshes. These all are soft and nonreflecting. Painting a realistic decoy is difficult. It is hard to imitate nature accurately, and only the master artists with years of research and experience can really do it effectively. Another problem associated with realistic painting is that a bird's plumage changes according to the seasons and mating periods. Furthermore, hens are often entirely different from drakes. The best way to begin is to refer to a good field guide in color.

A number of companies are now making special decoy-painting kits available. These include detailed drawings providing paint-by-the-numbers instructions and the premixed color paints. (See illustration 148.) This example, with step-by-step instructions, approaches the realistic coloring as done by professional carver/painter decoyists. Other drawings indicating feather details and painting schemes are included at the end of this chapter.

PAINTS Two kinds of paint are normally used by most decoyists. These are oil and acrylic. The procedures that follow here deal with acrylics. Some carvers prefer to use oils, because they blend easily and are more forgiving. They dry slowly and can simply be wiped off if a look isn't satisfactory. The novice carver should experiment with both oils and acrylics to determine which is best for his own technique. Acrylics are neat, easily mixed (on a plastic jar cover), they dry fast, blend well, and clean up with water. They are available at most art supply houses. Another feature of acrylics is that it is easier to paint white over black. Incidentally, remember that all paints dry a little darker than when first applied.

PREPARATIONS If the decoy has been feather burned, clean the surfaces with a semistiff brush to remove all excess residue (charring). An old toothbrush is perfect for this job. Seal the entire surface with a mixture of half varnish and half turpentine. Next, undercoat. This should be done in one of two ways, depending upon the condition of the surface. If the surface has been textured by burning, use a wet wash. This is a watered-down acrylic paint color-mixed to approximately match the intended top coat. If

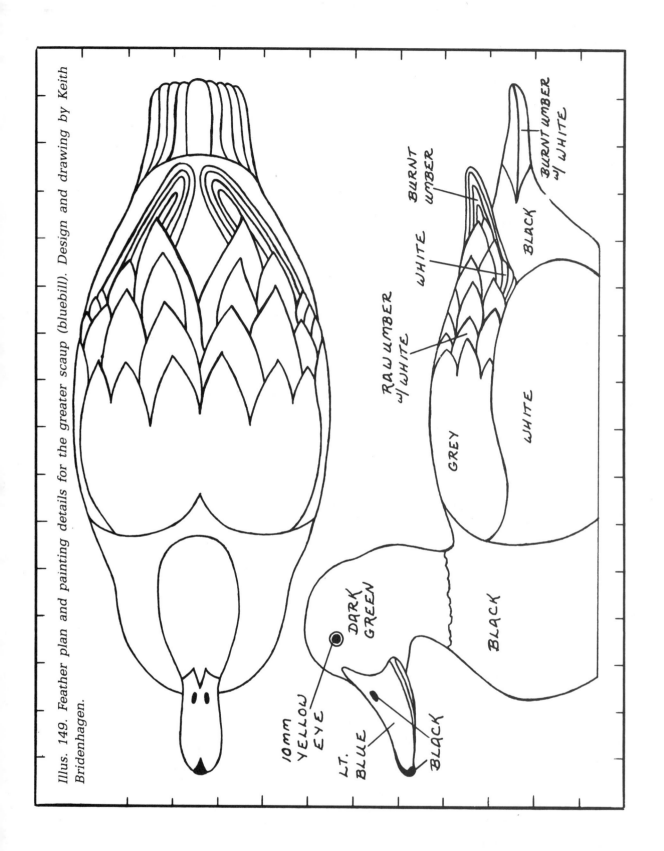

Illus. 149. Feather plan and painting details for the greater scaup (bluebill). Design and drawing by Keith Bridenhagen.

BURNT UMBER
w/ WHITE

BURNT
UMBER

WHITE

BLACK

RAW UMBER
w/ WHITE

GREY

WHITE

BLACK

DARK
GREEN

10mm
YELLOW
EYE

LT.
BLUE

BLACK

the surface is smooth and untextured apply an undercoat of gesso, which is a heavy-consistency paint containing white pigment and ground-up marble. It is available at any paint shop and is used to give surface texture. It is cleaned up or thinned out with water.

PAINTING THE GREATER SCAUP DRAKE (BLUEBILL) (This example is shown in a drawing, illustration 149, here, and in photos, illustrations 134–136, on pages 96–98.) The procedure, step by step, is as follows:

1. Paint the chest area, rump, and undersides of the wings black.

2. Paint the sides white.

3. Paint the secondary and tertial wing feathers raw umber with a little white added.

4. Paint the wing primaries burnt umber.

5. Mix burnt umber with a little white, and paint the tail feathers as demonstrated in illustration 150.

6. Paint the small secondary feathers white.

7. Next, paint the scapular area. Use a light grey (mixing black and white). Note: When mixing any special colors be sure to mix enough to do all parts of the bird. Greys are especially difficult to mix and match to the same shade.

8. Paint the head dark green. Mix green and black to achieve the appropriate color. (You can also add a touch of thalo bronze to give the head a slight iridescence.

9. Paint the inside of the nostrils black.

Illus. 150. Painting Bridenhagen's greater scaup drake. Note how the decoy is set upon a block so any surface can by painted conveniently.

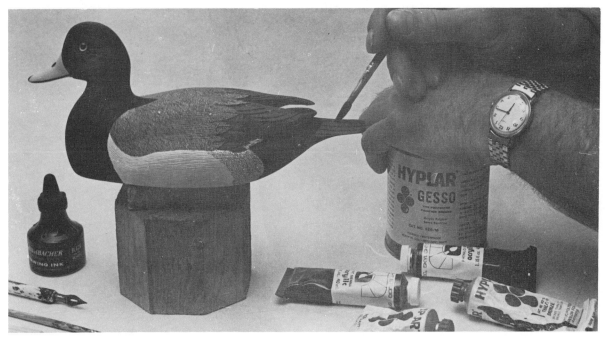

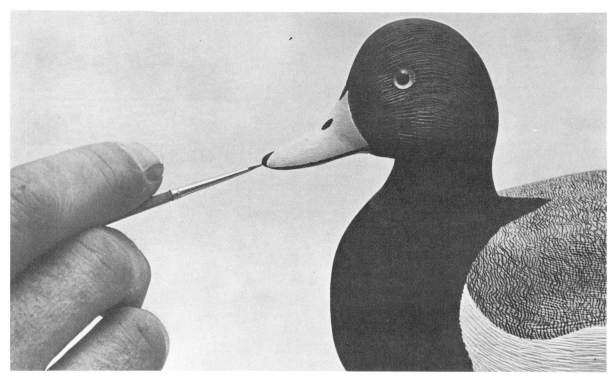

Illus. 151. Painting the nail.

Illus. 152. Vermiculations. These are thin wavy lines drawn with a fine pen and waterproof India ink.

10. Paint the bill a light blue (mixing blue and white). Remember that a thicker-consistency paint will dry somewhat more glossy than a wetter one. You want a little gloss on the bill.

11. Paint a black line on the bill to separate the mandibles. Paint the "nail" on the end of the bill black. (See illustration 151.)

12. This is an optional step. Vermiculation is an effective technique to give a more realistic, soft-feathered, impressionistic look to certain areas. This look is achieved by drawing thin wavy lines over solid, light-colored areas using a pen and waterproof India ink. Illustration 152 shows a good close-up of this interesting technique.

13. Sign your name to the bottom, and date it. Then sit back, enjoy, and let others admire your decoy.

VERMICULATION AREAS for some puddle and diving ducks are also included here for your reference.

Puddle-Duck Vermiculations

Mallard drake—sides and back scapulars

Pintail drake—entire buff area of sides and back

American widgeon drake—back extending to the tertials and sides, excluding the flank

Wood duck drake—sides

Green-winged teal drake—sides and upper back

Shovellers—rusty parts of sides

Diving-Duck Vermiculations

Red drake—sides and back

Canvasback drake—sides and back including scapulars, secondaries, and tertials

Greater scaup drake (bluebill)—back and flank

Lesser scaup drake—back, flank, and sides

Ring-necked drake—grey sides

Merganser Vermiculations

Hooded merganser drake—gold sides

Red-breasted merganser—sides and rump

SOME ADDITIONAL TIPS Wherever one batch of color coincides with another, for example, where the chest meets the side, make the colors appear to run together somewhat. In short, use jagged, irregular lines so you do not have sharply separated areas of color. In reality, the various feathering areas of a duck do not have abrupt, uniform demarcations.

OTHER DECOY PLANS Designs and drawings developed by Keith Bridenhagen that give feathering and paint-color details for some popular decoys are as follows: Mallard drake, illustration 153; mallard hen, illustration 154; pintail drake, illustration 155; canvasback drake, illustration 156; and a Canadian goose, illustration 157. The lines bordering these plans are divided at every inch (for grid locations), to aid in redrawing to full size for patterns.

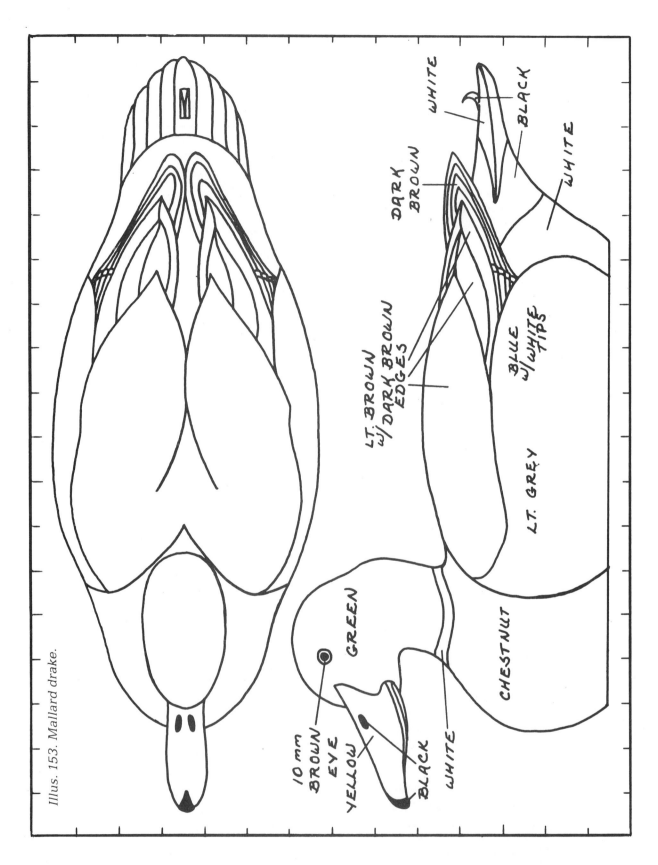

Illus. 153. Mallard drake.

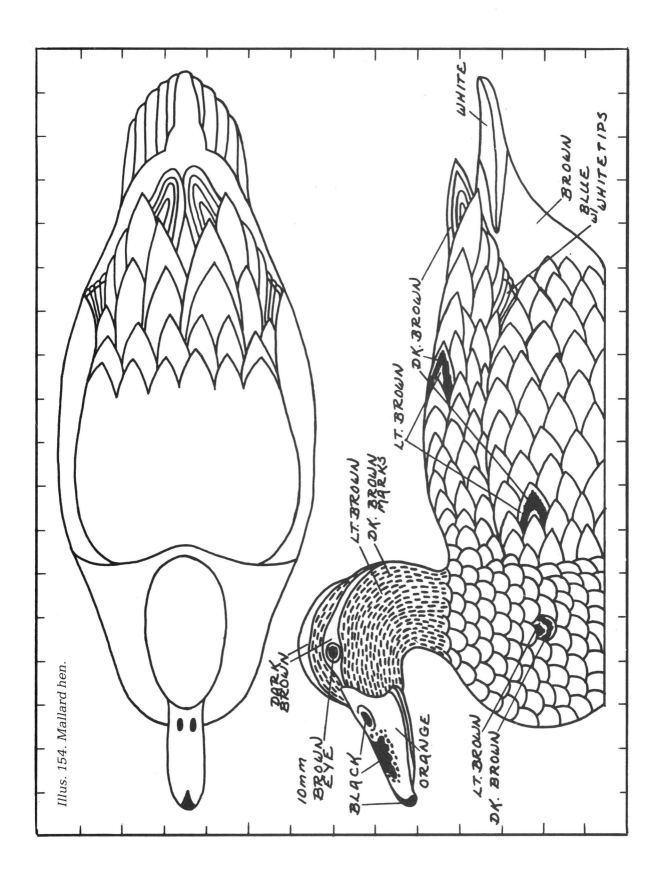

Illus. 154. Mallard hen.

WHITE

BROWN

BLUE w/WHITE TIPS

DK. BROWN

LT. BROWN

LT. BROWN
DK. BROWN MARKS

DARK BROWN

10mm
BROWN
EYE

BLACK

ORANGE

LT. BROWN

DK. BROWN

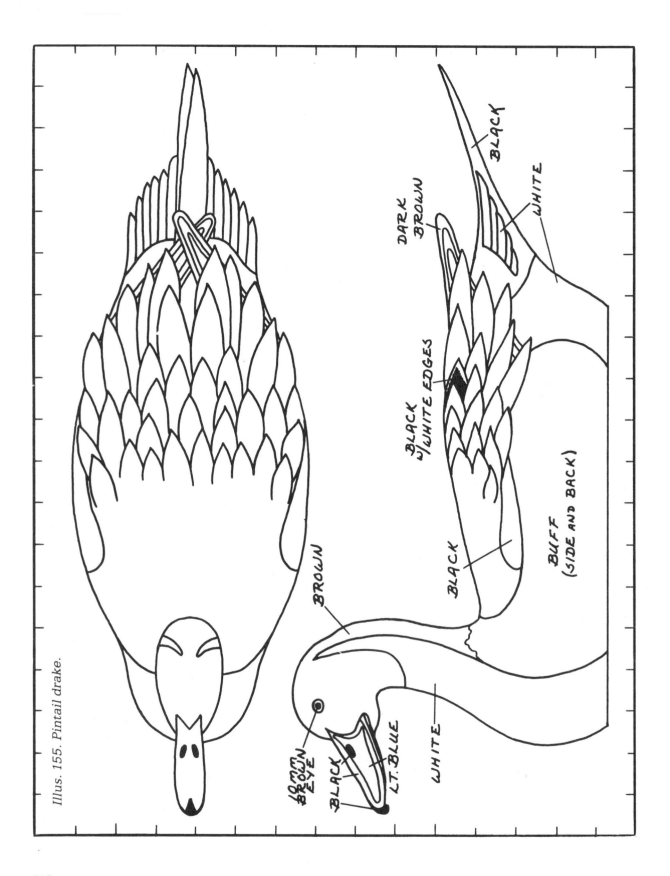

Illus. 155. Pintail drake.

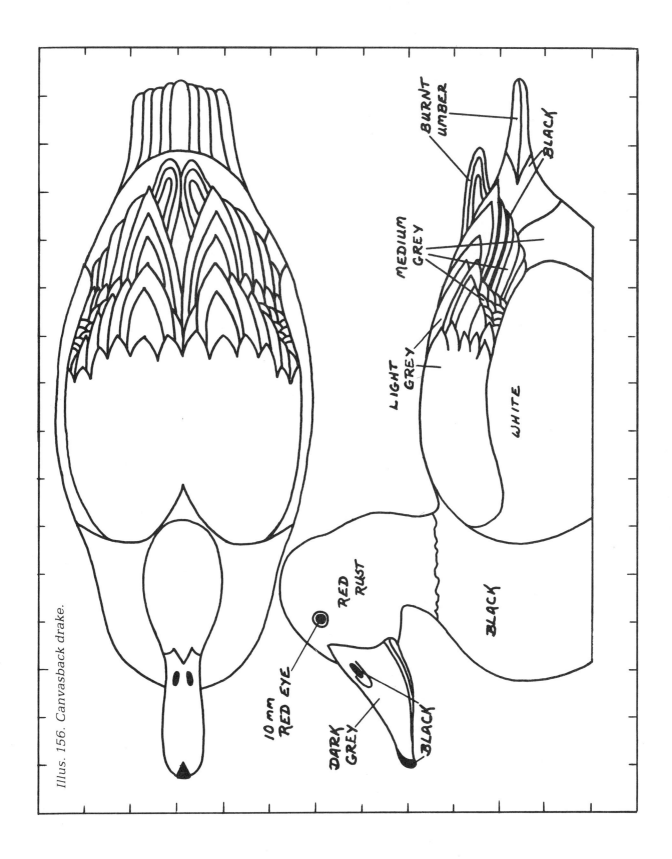

Illus. 156. Canvasback drake.

BURNT UMBER

BLACK

MEDIUM GREY

LIGHT GREY

WHITE

BLACK

10 mm RED EYE

RED RUST

DARK GREY

BLACK

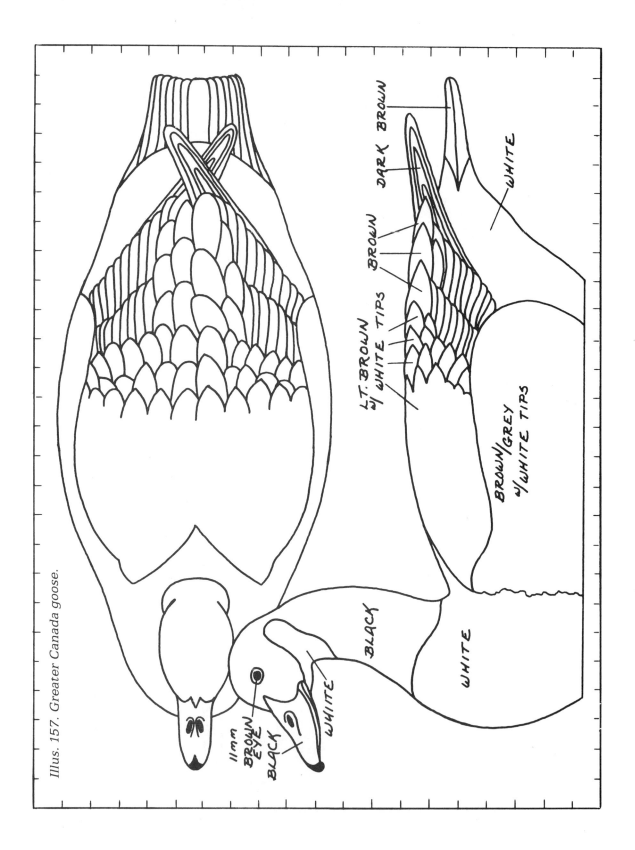

Illus. 157. Greater Canada goose.

DARK BROWN

WHITE

BROWN

LT. BROWN
w/ WHITE TIPS

BROWN/GREY
w/WHITE TIPS

BLACK

WHITE

11mm
BROWN
EYE

BLACK

WHITE

GLASS EYES Various eye sizes and colors are recommended for the decoys described in this book. (See illustration 158.)

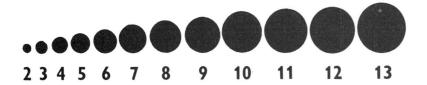

2 3 4 5 6 7 8 9 10 11 12 13

Illus. 158. Full-size glass eyes. Specify orders by diameters (in millimeters) and color.

EYE SIZE AND COLOR CHART

Species	Size in mm	Color	Species	Size in mm	Color
Bald pate (Widgeon)	10	Yellow	Pintail	9	Brown
Black duck	10	Black	Plover	6	Brown
Bluebill (Greater scaup)	10	Yellow	*Red head	10	Yellow
Bluebill (Lesser scaup)	11	Yellow	+ Ring-necked duck	10	Straw
Bufflehead	10	Brown	Ruddy	11	Hazel
Canvasback	10	Red	Sandpiper	6 or 7	Brown
Eider	11	Brown	Scoter	10	White
Eider, Spectacled	11	White	Scoter, Black	10	Brown
Florida	11	Brown	*Scoter, Surf	10	White
Gadwell	11	Brown	Scoter, White-winged	10	Straw
Goldeneye	11	Yellow	Shell drake	10	Red
Goose	12	Brown	Shoveller	10	Yellow
Harlequin	10	Brown	Snipe	6 or 7	Brown
Loon	14	Red	Spoonbill	10	Yellow
Mallard	11	Brown	Teal, Blue-wing	9	Brown
Merganser, American	11	Red	*Teal, Cinnamon	9	Red
Merganser, Hooded	9	Yellow	Teal, Green-wing	9	Hazel
Merganser, Red-Breasted	11	Red	Widgeon (Bald pate)	10	Yellow
Old-squaw	10	Brown	*Wood duck	11	Red

*Female takes brown
+ Female takes hazel

8

Working Decoys Simplified

Primarily for economic reasons, most hunters today use ready-made decoys made of lightweight plastics. These can be purchased at ridiculously low prices, ranging from $15 to $35 per dozen. They cost much less than what a decoy carver usually pays for just his wood. So why do duck shooters still make their own decoys? First of all, some feel that making decoys is actually a very important part of the sport itself. Others simply have a certain affection for wood decoys because of their traditional quality.

Duck hunters are often said to be a peculiar bunch when it comes to their prized bird lures. They have specific ideas regarding what is exactly the right look or floating action necessary to attract birds to their own hunting regions. This particular sort of hunter may not be able to find exactly what he needs and wants, so he makes his own. Along with all these reasons for making decoys is the ever-existing potential for that extra glow of satisfaction when you bag your limit shooting over your very own, handmade decoys.

The working decoy is functional only. This sounds simple at first, but there are many contributing factors to consider when creating a decoy to look and perform exactly as you want it to. Decorative decoys are only ornaments made for humans to look at. Working decoys are made to perform. They must attract and lure birds to a specific spot that looks safe and welcome in the eyes of the "traveller." So, how does one make working decoys with all of these tangible qualities and requirements? Exactly what it is that magically constitutes a good working decoy is the subject of a much-disputed, never-ending controversy even today, just as it has been over the years. The debate goes way back to the days when market hunters, shooting not for sport but money, relied heavily on their decoys for taking hundreds of ducks daily. This distasteful occupation was abruptly ended in the United States by the Migratory Bird Treaty Act of 1913, in cooperation with the

Canadian Government. Birds are now only hunted for sport during short authorized seasons, and the sale of game birds is strictly forbidden.

Over the years there have evolved several fundamental and obvious things duck shooters pretty well agree on. The decoy should be carved to a fairly close facsimile of the desired species in form, contour, and size. (See illustrations 159 and 160.) Some, however, insist that the decoy should be oversized. Decoys should also be engineered to float realistically on the water. They need to be painted soft colors and especially be nonglossy, nonreflecting, and nonshiny, even when wet. For practical reasons, decoys should be lightweight, yet durable and tough enough to be handled roughly without breaking. Most decoyists agree that it is just impractical to put a lot of effort into excessive detail work. Design profiles are often simplified to embody strength and durability. For example, the fragile raised or fanned-out feathers and long delicate tail feathers typical of some species are often eliminated or restyled for strength. The head to body joint is always strengthened with a dowel and glue.

Working decoys have evolved from two basic construction methods: solid body and hollow body. The solid-body decoys are viewed by many historians and collectors as the best type ever made. (See illustrations 159 and 160.)

Illus. 159. Working bluebill decoys of solid one-piece-body construction by John Eriksson. Female above, male below. Note the comb-textured vermiculation on the back of the male. A heavy layer of grey paint just starting to set was worked in irregular-line fashion and wiped with a rag. The procedure was then repeated.

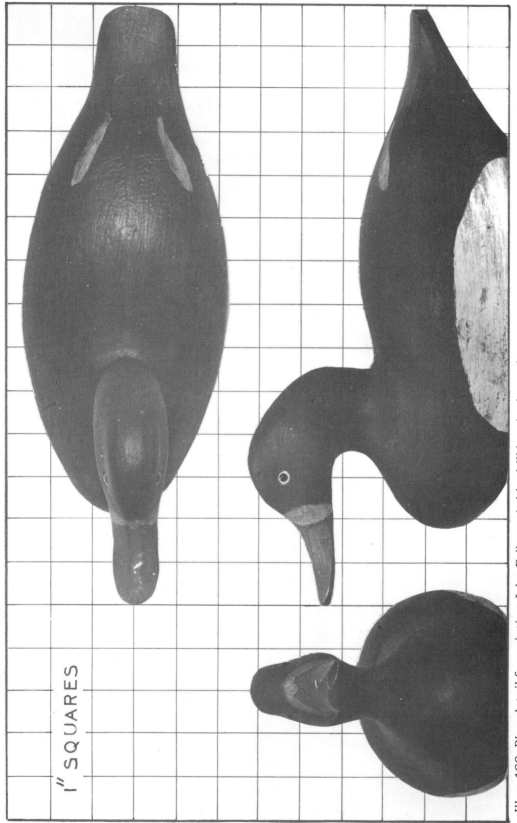

1" SQUARES

Illus. 160. Plan detail for painting John Eriksson's bluebill hen is shown here.

The early solid-body decoys were made of seasoned (air-dried) white cedar. In Canada, the American Midwest, and most of the Great Lakes areas, the solid, one-piece-body decoys are still considered the best. On the other hand, hollow-body decoy construction originated in the eastern United States, and this method is also believed by many to be the best technique. (See illustrations 161 and 162.) Refer to Chapters 4 and 5 for information about shaping, done to fashion the simple decorative decoy. Remember, bodies need not be precisely shaped, fine sanding is not required, and, in a sense, the block can be more crude looking, and thus more quickly carved than other kinds of decoys.

Texturing of working decoys is usually simulated by painting and not done by carving or burning. The emphasis is on simplification of the major features which normally accent a particular species. Working decoys can also be categorized as either puddle or diving ducks. To simplify making a broad range of decoys (having distinctive configurations and expressive features for each different species), the job can be reduced to two basic body styles, one for diving ducks (illustration 162) and one for puddle ducks (illustration 161). Different heads are attached to the one body design for puddle ducks from those attached to the one body design representative of most diving ducks. To further simplify the making of working decoys two basic painting plans are also given: one for diving ducks and one for puddle ducks. (See illustration 163.) This simplification is based upon the generally accepted theory that a basic decoy similar in appearance to a bluebill will attract any of the other species of diving ducks. A basic decoy representative of a mallard will essentially attract all of the other species of puddle ducks. Glass eyes can be installed as previously described or the eyes just painted on.

Some general suggestions to keep in mind when making working decoys are included here:

MATERIAL CHOICES Lightweight, strong woods, such as white cedar, pine, or cypress are all good. White cedar has a natural resistance to moisture and weather checking.

ASSEMBLY Use good waterproof glues. Epoxy is highly recommended. Resorcinol and marine-grade plastic resins are just a little less suitable, with the latter being the most economical. If hollowing bodies, be sure to seal the inside surfaces of the hollowed-out area to make a waterproof barrier. Use epoxy paint or a good exterior paint or enamel over a generous sealer coat of boiled linseed oil. Be sure that all holes, cracks, and other voids are carefully filled on all decoys, especially hollow-body decoys. You don't want the hollow cavity to fill with water. Plywood of exterior- or marine-grade makes a good base for hollow-body decoys. (See illustrations 161 and 162.) Be sure to fill and seal any voids in the plywood-edge plies. Use brass screws for the final assembly, but wait—be sure to check flotation qualities before permanently attaching the base and the keel.

Illus. 161. Puddle duck decoys simplified. Here, only one body shape is used with different heads. Hollowing and keel sizes are optional. Drawing by Keith Bridenhagen.

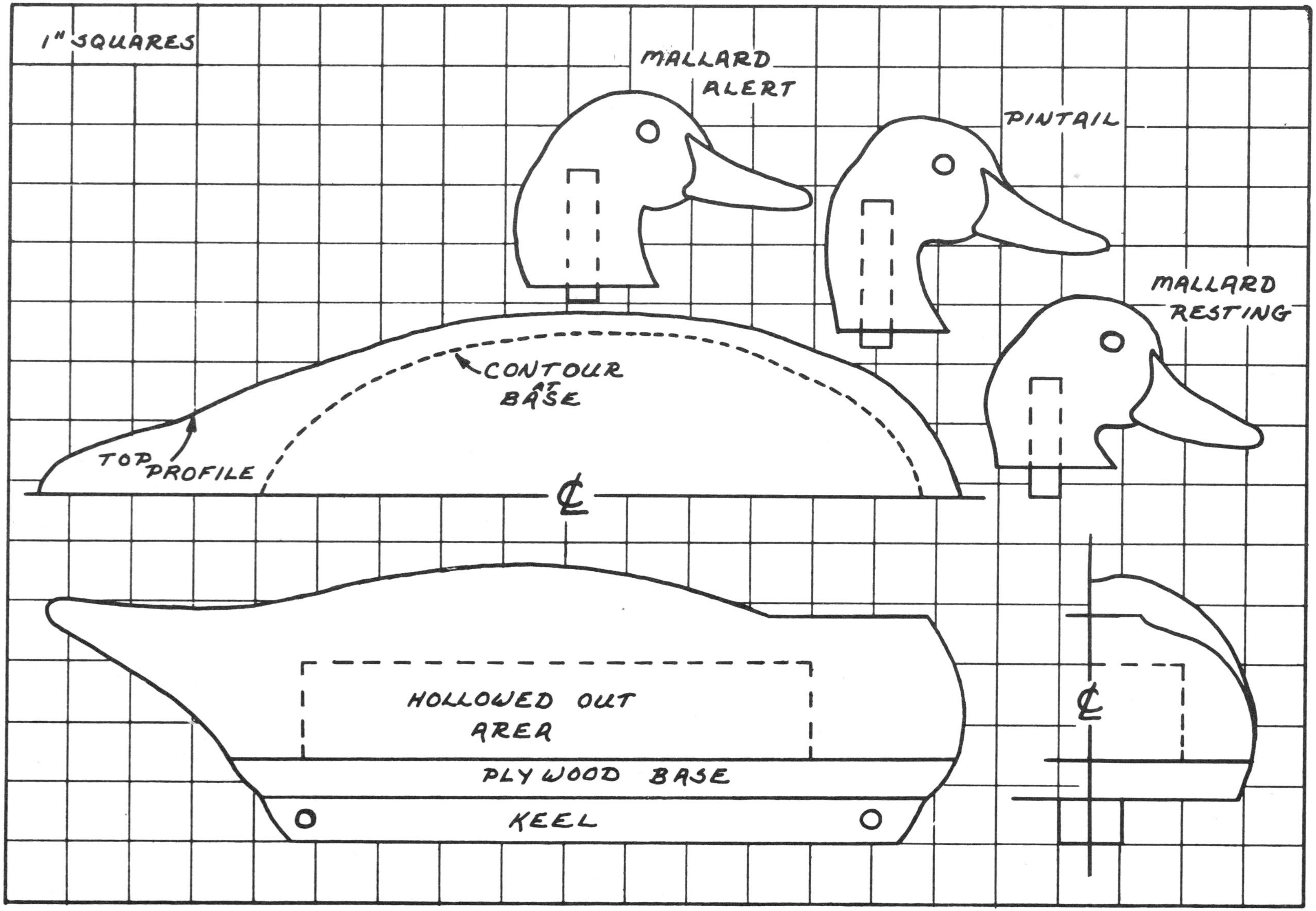

1" SQUARES

PINTAIL

MALLARD RESTING

MALLARD ALERT

CONTOUR AT BASE

TOP PROFILE

HOLLOWED OUT AREA

PLYWOOD BASE

KEEL

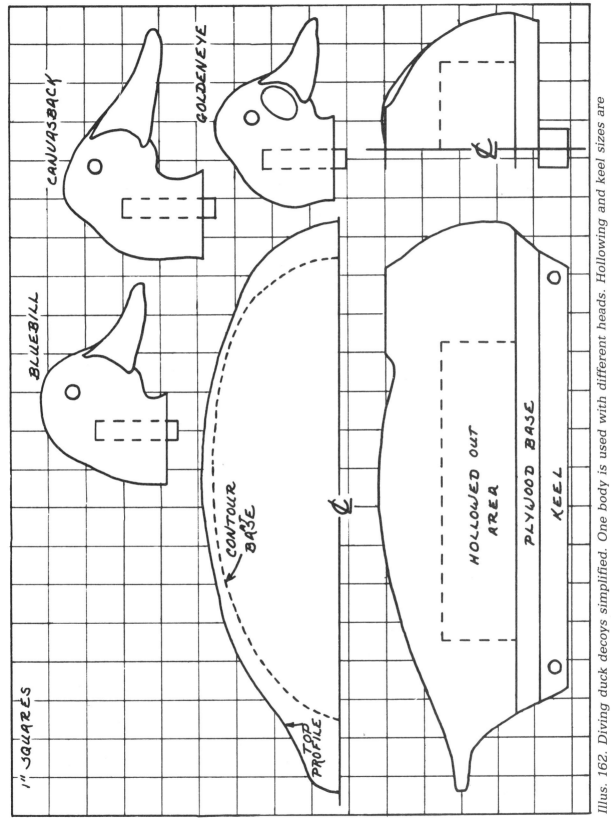

1" SQUARES

CANVASBACK

GOLDENEYE

BLUEBILL

CONTOUR BASE

TOP PROFILE

HOLLOWED OUT AREA

PLYWOOD BASE

KEEL

Illus. 162. Diving duck decoys simplified. One body is used with different heads. Hollowing and keel sizes are optional. Drawing by Keith Bridenhagen.

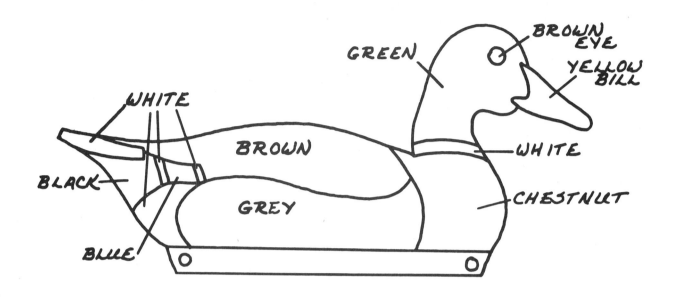

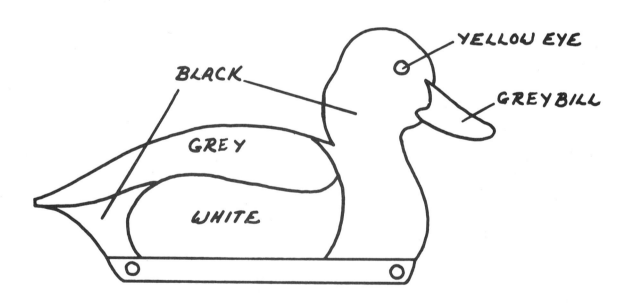

Illus. 163. Simplified painting details for puddle ducks, above, and diving ducks, below. Drawings by Keith Bridenhagen.

KEELS, WEIGHTS, AND FLOTATION A keel keeps the decoy from drifting randomly about in various directions. The keel works to counteract surface breezes and currents. The bigger the body of water the decoy will sit in, the deeper the keel should be so the decoy can ride waves without toppling over. Decoy makers usually add weights to the bottoms of the keels to lower the center of gravity. This adds stability to the decoy. Weights counterbalance the decoy. Depending upon the amount of weight added, they determine how deeply the body sits down into the water and how much of the decoy profile is left exposed above the water. Some ducks appear to float lower in the water than others, so this is of major significance to get a realistic look.

A really good decoy is able to right itself from any position. If it is toppled over by wave or wind, it will set itself back upright. This requires some experimentation. If the beam (body width) is too narrow, or if the body is too high, the decoy will be tippy. Other things can cause tippy decoys, too: for example, the keel may be too narrow, or the decoy may not be properly weighted.

Weights are usually pieces of sheet lead attached to the bottom of the keel with screws. Be sure that weights are not placed too far forward or too far toward the rear. Also a definite relationship should exist between the tail height and the surface of the water. Another consideration to observe is the action that the anchor line has on the flotation of the decoy. Maybe the weight has to be set back to counterbalance the downward tug or pull of the anchor line. Incidentally, the anchor line can be attached to either the front or rear of the keel. Thus, when setting out your rig on water with currents, not all the ducks will be facing the same direction and you'll have a more natural mooring. The anchor line is usually at least three times as long as the depth of the water.

In order to get all these forces working just right, test your decoy in water. Make your test in a bathtub or something similar. Do not fasten the keel and weights permanently until after making the test. Tape them on, or hold them in position with rubber bands for the flotation test. By adjusting the weight location you can observe and eventually improve flotation by trial and error. It may be necessary to consider a heavier, denser wood, such as oak or maple, for the keel. If the decoy floats too high, add more weight or reduce the beam by shaving off the sides of the body. If it floats too low, remove weight, hollow it out more, or increase the beam. Some decoyists, who pride themselves on perfection, cut special cavities in their keels (with slanted, dovetail-like sides). Then they pour in melted lead, to make a neater overall job. In such cases, hardwood keels are best as they withstand the immense heat of the hot lead until it cools.

Finally, when the problems of weights, keels, and flotation have been overcome, assemble everything with good waterproof glue and brass wood screws.

PAINTING AND DETAILING In general, the painting should be a little more conspicuous than the natural camouflaging colors of real birds. After all, the object is to attract with the decoy, not to hide. Check illustration 163 for the basic painting patterns. These are overly simplified, but adequate. Add your own ideas and perceptions as you wish. Just remember to use flat, dull colors. Paints of thicker consistency are recommended. They don't run, and they allow you to employ some texturing techniques.

Oil paints with a flat alkyd base and acrylics are widely used. For painted decoys details can be simulated in numerous ways, including many of the age-old techniques of wire brushing, scratch coating, comb texturing, stippling, dry-brush work, and so on. The emphasis is on simplification.

Paint the base coat after a good sealer has been applied, such as boiled linseed oil. Paint the major color areas first. Experiment using brush stippling techniques to simulate vermiculation. The dry-brush method is good for blending color areas. Pull the brush lightly over the freshly applied paint, working from the head toward the rear. This gives a nice look, simulating soft feather ends.

The scratch technique is a simple, quick method using a blunt object such as a nail (illustration 164) or comb. (See illustration 159.) Remember, the decoy is painted for distance viewing, which tends to simplify and consolidate details. Elegant detailing is solely for the benefit and pride of the maker, not to lure ducks. Some of the earliest decoys were not even painted at all and they were surprisingly effective. Some hunters only torched their decoys, in which case they used pitchy pine to help seal the wood. Others simply dipped their decoys in a container of creosote, a dark preservative.

Illus. 164. Simplified techniques to simulate feathering details during painting. Left: Scratch method for head feathers. Right: Stamp method for painting feather borders using felt rolled around a round object. (Drawings adapted from painting instructions provided by Parker Paint Co.)

Two simple, traditional detail methods easily employed without much time or effort are illustrated in illustration 164. In such methods allow the base coat to dry hard. The second coat is scratched off with a blunt instrument such as a nail or a 1"–1½" (2.54 cm–3.8 cm) piece of a coarse hair comb. The scratching is usually done just when the top coat starts to stiffen during drying. These techniques allow the base color to show through. The nail-scratch technique is good for neck- and head-feather simulation. The comb method is good for simulating texture on vermiculated areas. (Refer again to illustration 159.)

Another simple technique is to stamp on feather borders. This is a particularly good technique for doing the mallard hen. It may be worth the effort to pencil out some feather shapes and locations first. The feather border imprint is made individually, feather by feather, using small pieces of old felt. The felt from an old, discarded felt hat works perfectly. Simply cut up small pieces and hold them around a round object, as shown in illustration 164. Fast feather borders are easily made by lightly moistening the edge of the felt with paint. Apply it to the decoy surface in the same manner you would use a rubber stamp.

The size of the feathers can be controlled by the length of felt and the diameter of the supporting stick. While the feather borders are still wet, with a dry brush very lightly pull the colors outward (working toward the tail) to soften the contrast.

Most of these techniques are old, traditional methods. Use them, along with your own creative imagination, to develop a style and technique to your own satisfaction.

Incidentally, anchor weights are needed before launching your decoys. Some people make or buy moulds and cast their own with lead. Weights can also be purchased very inexpensively from most sports shops that handle store-bought decoys.

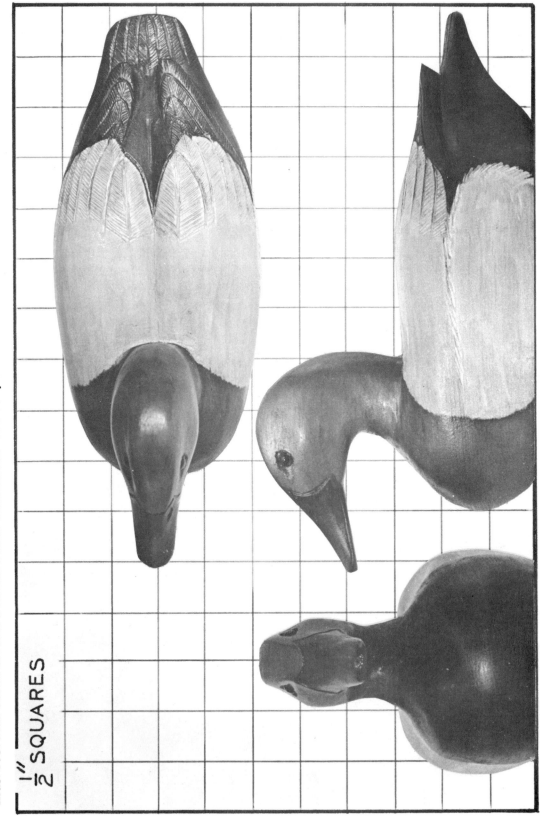

Illus. 165. Plan detail of Peter Bosman's mini-canvasback. The body could be carved from a 2 × 4 (5 × 10 cm).

$\frac{1''}{2}$ SQUARES

9

Gallery of Decoys

On the pages that follow are a generous selection of illustrations showing typical decoys made by prominent professional carvers from the Door County, Wisconsin, area. Displayed here are works of Peter Bosman, Keith Bridenhagen, Bill Dehos, John Eriksson, Thomas Herlache, and Harold Schopf. You will find this helpful exhibit a handy reference for making your own wood decoys. Each of the exhibited works reveals the artist's own individualized method and style. Viewing and studying this collective and varied display of photographs and plans should provide you with a good overall basis for establishing your own standards and goals.

The decoy sculptures in this chapter include decoys from very basic to extremely complex, from small to large, from simple decorative decoys to advanced realistic ones with part- or full-feather texturing. Also included are those with basic natural finishes, as well as those that are realistically painted. Where advantageous, included are extra views or photographic close-ups—so interesting or complicated details can be more clearly observed and understood.

Illus. 166. This mini-decoy canvasback by Peter Bosman is an excellent beginning decoy.

Illus. 167. A stylized pintail in wormy butternut by Bill Dehos. Although carved entirely from one block of wood, it could be carved from two pieces— one for the head and one for the body.

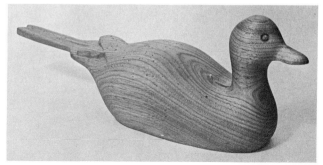

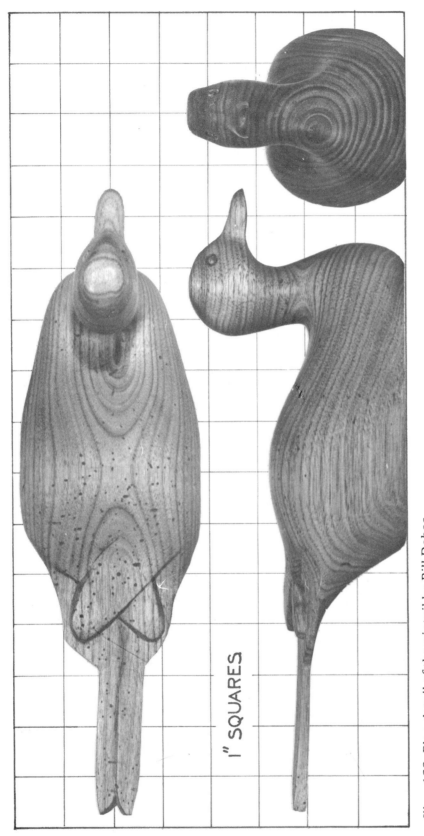

1" SQUARES

Illus. 168. Plan detail of the pintail by Bill Dehos.

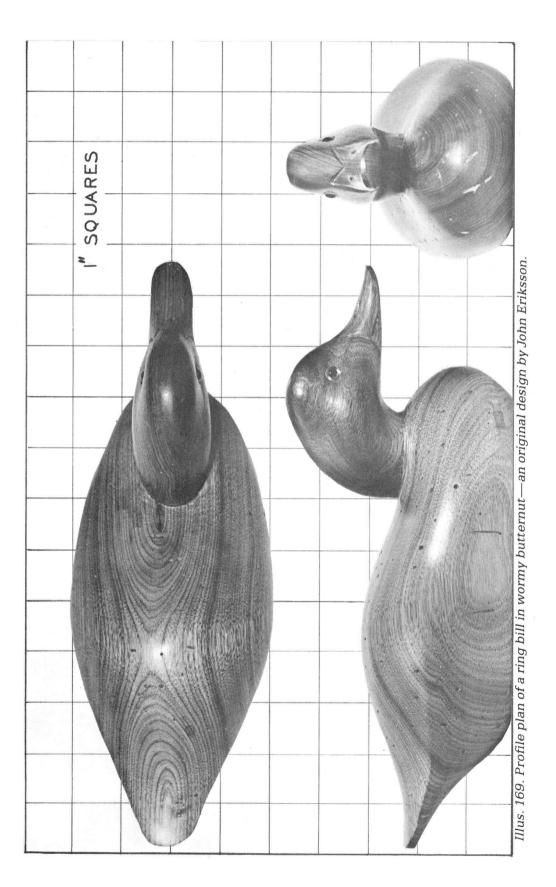

Illus. 169. Profile plan of a ring bill in wormy butternut—an original design by John Eriksson.

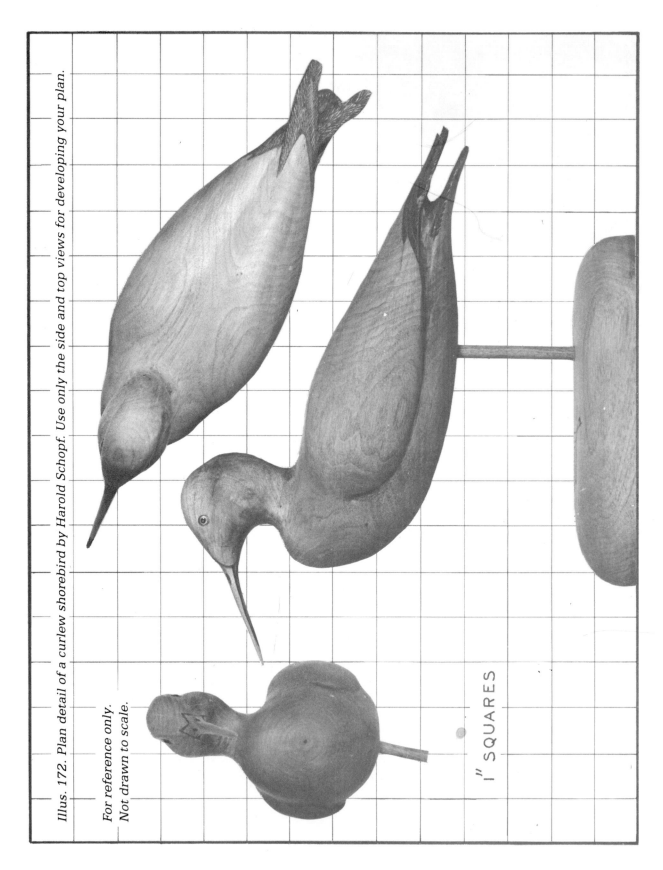

Illus. 172. Plan detail of a curlew shorebird by Harold Schopf. Use only the side and top views for developing your plan.

For reference only.
Not drawn to scale.

1" SQUARES

Illus. 173. Head close-up of the curlew. The beak is a ⅜-inch (9.5-mm) birch dowel fit into the head and then carved.

Illus. 174. Tail-feathering detail.

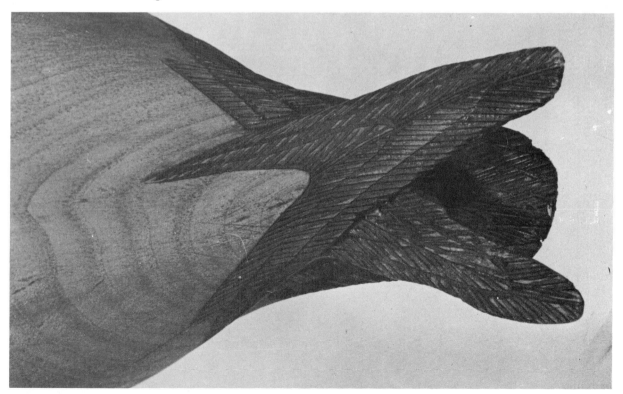

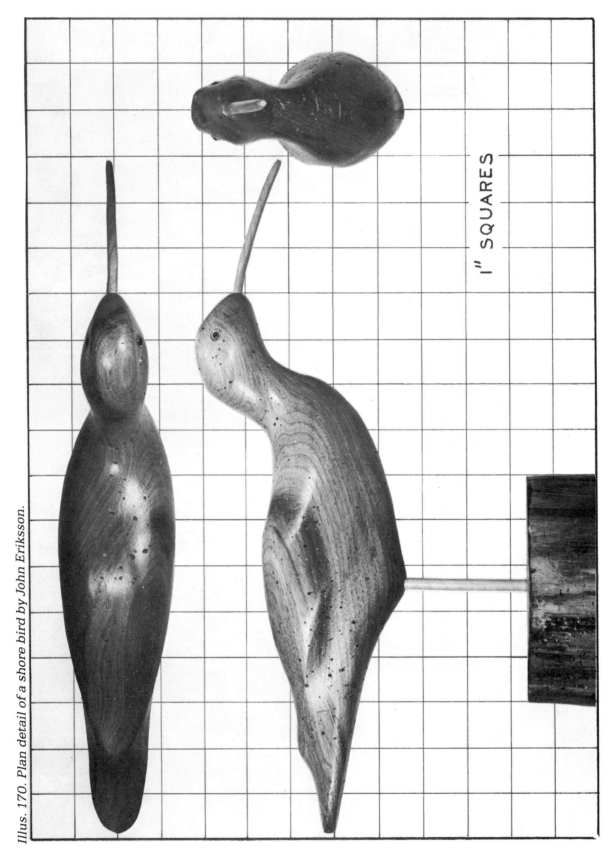

Illus. 170. Plan detail of a shore bird by John Eriksson.

1" SQUARES

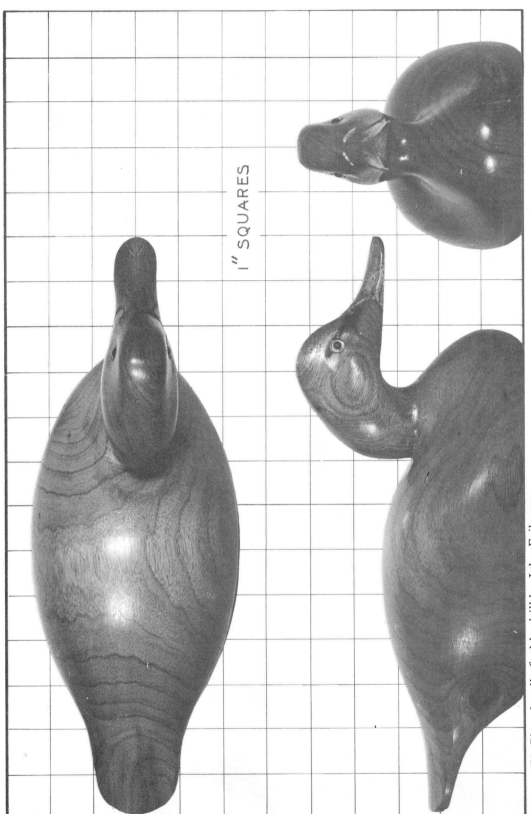

1" SQUARES

Illus. 171. Plan detail of a bluebill by John Eriksson.

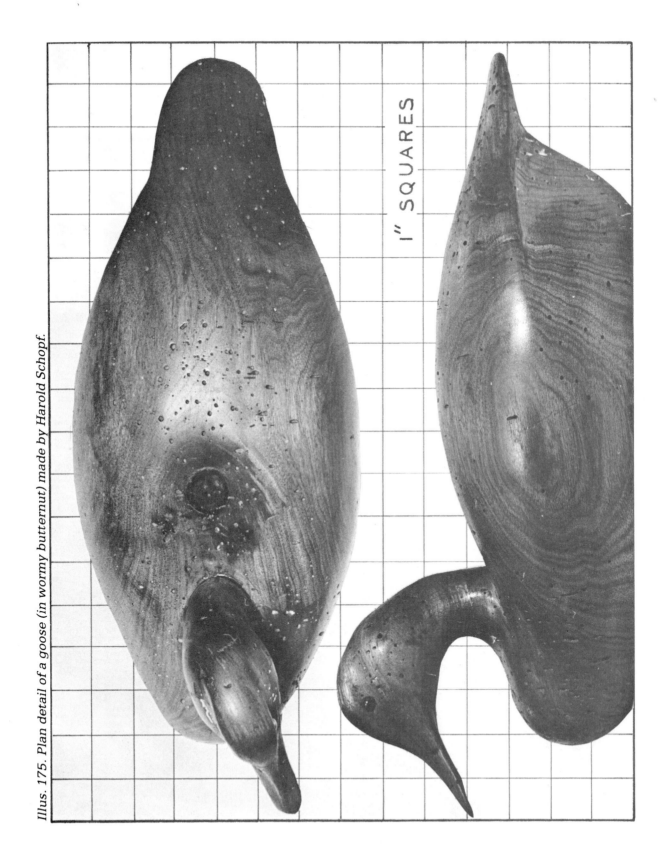

Illus. 175. Plan detail of a goose (in wormy butternut) made by Harold Schopf.

1" SQUARES

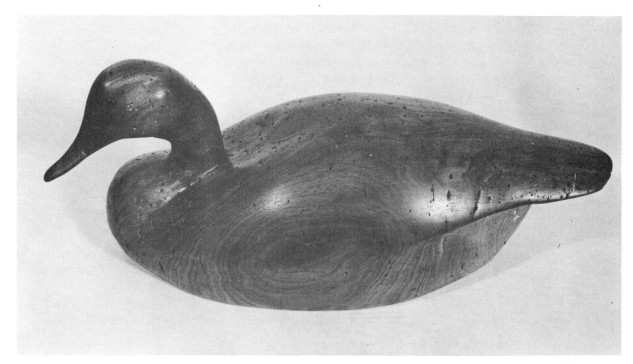

Illus. 176.

Illus. 177.

Illus. 178.

Illus. 175–178. Different views of the goose.

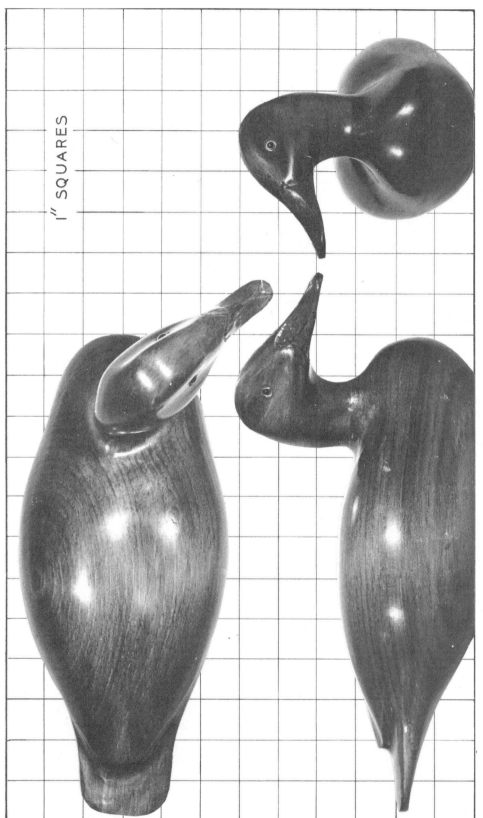

1″ SQUARES

Illus. 179. Plan detail of a canvasback in stained pine by John Eriksson.

Illus. 180. Head detail.

Illus. 181. Profile-view of the canvasback.

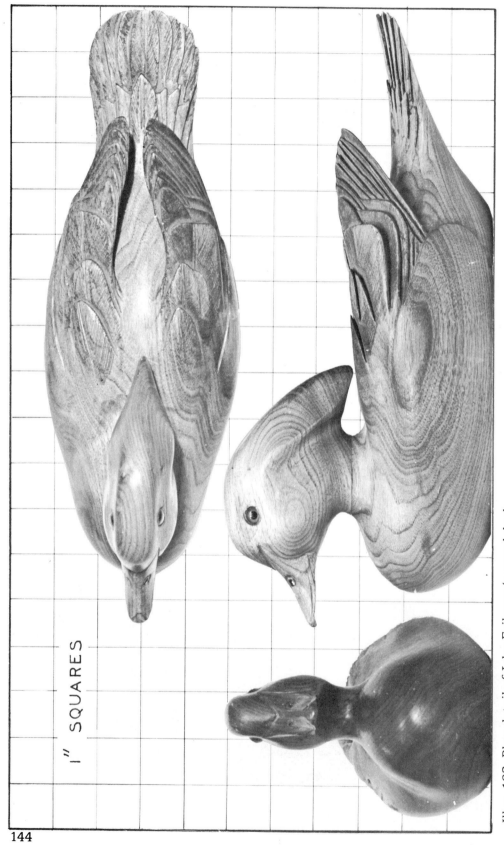

1" SQUARES

Illus. 182. Plan detail of John Eriksson's wood duck.

Illus. 182–185. Various views of John Eriksson's wood duck.

Illus. 183.

Illus. 184.

Illus. 185.

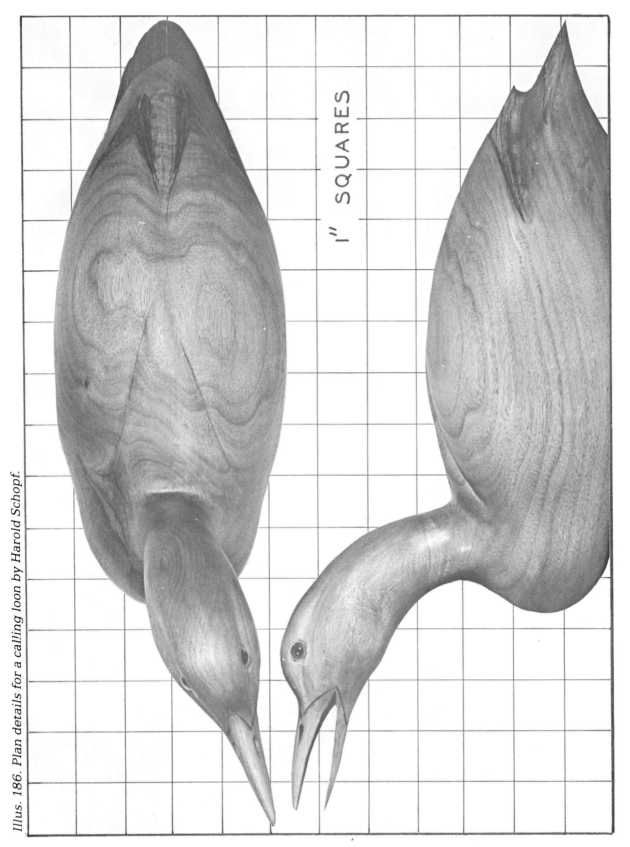

1" SQUARES

Illus. 186. Plan details for a calling loon by Harold Schopf.

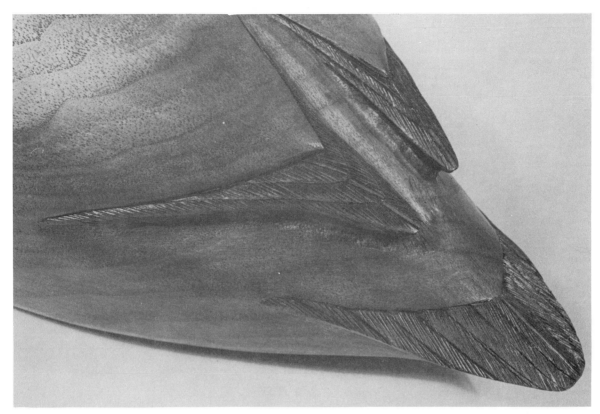

Illus. 187.

Illus. 187–189. Close-up details of the calling loon. The mouth was made by boring a ⅜-inch (9.5-mm) hole straight into the bill before shaping the bill.

Illus. 188.

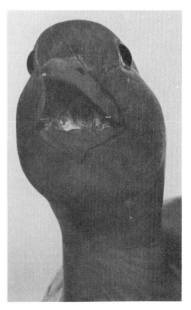

Illus. 190. Plan detail of John Eriksson's mallard drake.

Illus. 191. Head close-up.

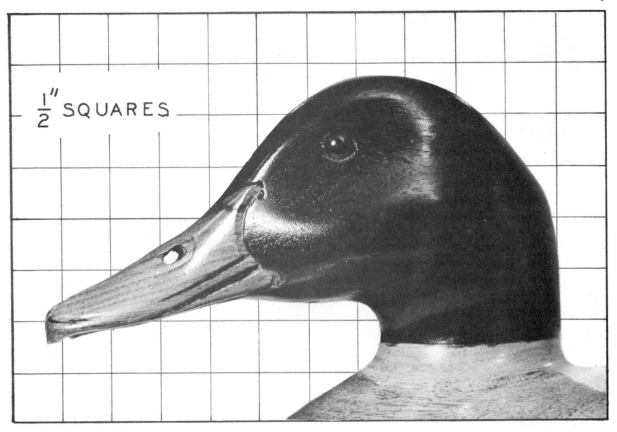

Illus. 192. The mallard drake carved from butternut, colored and finished with transparent stain (food coloring) mixed with Deft clear wood finish.

Illus. 193. Close-up of the carved feathering.

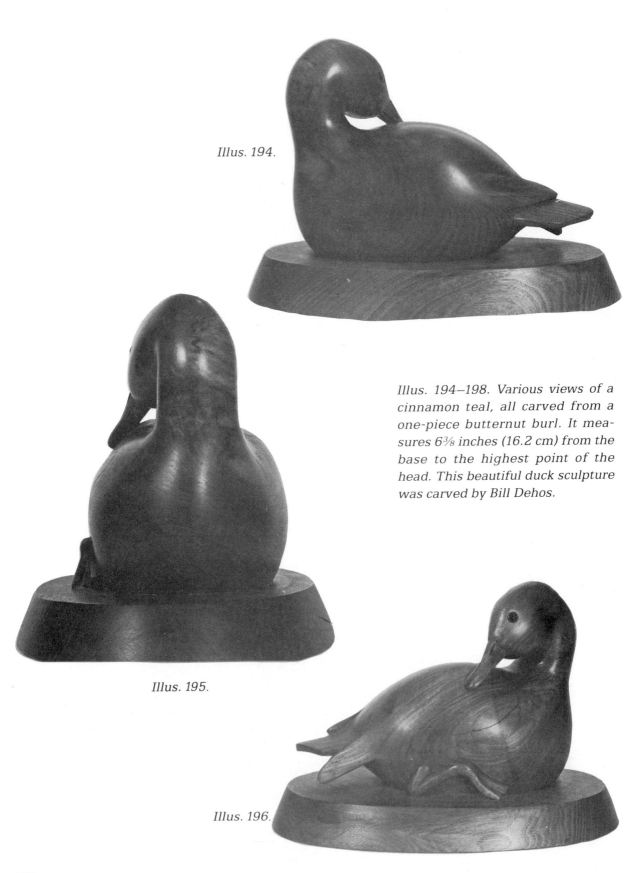

Illus. 194.

Illus. 194–198. Various views of a cinnamon teal, all carved from a one-piece butternut burl. It measures 6⅜ inches (16.2 cm) from the base to the highest point of the head. This beautiful duck sculpture was carved by Bill Dehos.

Illus. 195.

Illus. 196.

Illus. 197.

Illus. 198.

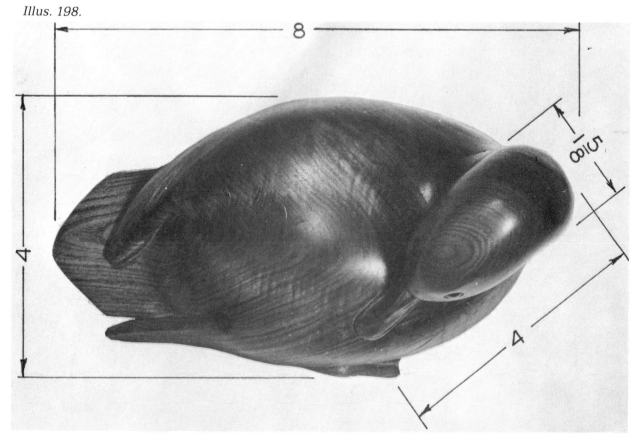

Illus. 199. Some views of a Canadian goose carved by John Eriksson. This full-sized decoy measures 29 inches (73.6 cm) in overall length, is 10 inches (25 cm) at the highest point (of the head), and is about 9 inches (23 cm) at the widest point of the body.

Illus. 200. Two-piece hollow-body bluebill of butternut by the author.

Illus. 201. Shoveller in cherry by Keith Bridenhagen.

Illus. 202. Green-wing teal drake in wormy butternut by Keith Bridenhagen.

Illus. 203. Old squaw drake in wormy butternut by Keith Bridenhagen.

Illus. 204. Teal in wormy butternut by John Eriksson.

Illus. 205. Hooded merganser hen by Keith Bridenhagen.

Illus. 206. Ruddy duck drake by Keith Bridenhagen.

Illus. 207. Mallard drake by Keith Bridenhagen

Illus. 208. Black-duck drake by Keith Bridenhagen.

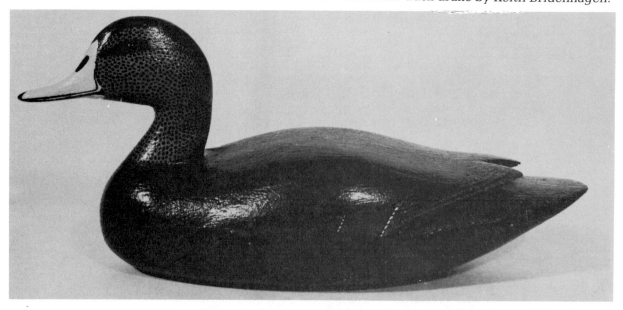

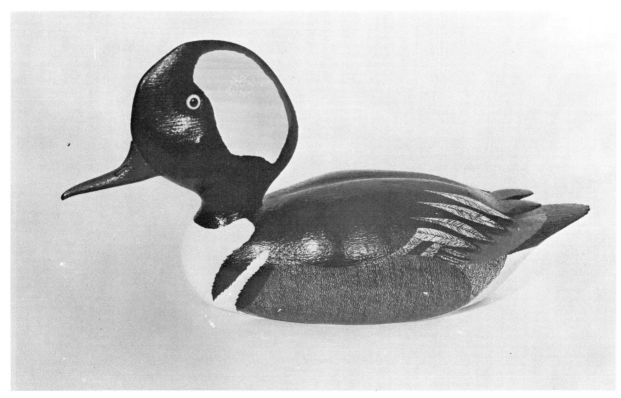

Illus. 209. Hooded merganser drake by Keith Bridenhagen.

Illus. 210. Canvasback drake by Keith Bridenhagen.

Illus. 211. Blue-wing teal drake by Keith Bridenhagen.

Illus. 212. Blue-wing teal drake by Thomas Herlache.

Illus. 213. Canadian goose by Harold Schopf.

Illus. 214. Wood ducks by Keith Bridenhagen.

Index